W9-BRC-803

# Praise for *Power Relationships*

"Relationships come about in different ways: Adversity, kindness, luck, planning, and humility can all play their part. Andrew and Jerry—in their inimitable style and with the credibility of experts in the field—illustrate practically and amusingly how relationships are created that are lasting and mutually beneficial."

**—Sir Win Bischoff, Chairman, Lloyds Banking Group**

*"Power Relationships* provides the perfect advice and examples on how to build relationships that truly work. It's an enjoyable read that will produce real results. I hope every person in Grant Thornton throughout the world reads the book, and that our competitors do not."

**—Ed Nusbaum, Global CEO, Grant Thornton International**

"Jerry and Andrew have written a book that unlocks the secret of relationship building. Relationships govern our personal world and everything we do. It is the zest in our life—with our family, colleagues, and clients. *Power Relationships* is the best-written book on the subject. I want all of our staff and employees to have a copy."

**—Mark Cummings, President and CEO, ScotiaLife Insurance Company**

"I wish everyone could read *Power Relationships*. It would be a better world. This book leads the way. It proves to me that if business is based only on monetary gain, you will not solve an issue without a fight. Read *Power Relationships* for the answer."

**—Alan Hassenfeld, Former CEO and Chairman of the Board, Hasbro, Inc.**

"Sobel and Panas have added real substance to the basic truth that success in life depends on relationships between people. One cannot hope to excel in sales, supervision, service, or personal growth without sensitivity to the 26 tenets that the authors identify and explain persuasively. The many short stories that illustrate the main points in this volume are a delight to read."

**—Richard Ekman, PhD, President, Council of Independent Colleges**

"If you believe your business should be all about the client, you'll find *Power Relationships* a truly powerful book. It clearly shows how to create win-wins with your most important clients and prospects."

**—Francesco Vanni d'Archirafi, CEO, Citi Holdings, Citigroup**

"I loved the laws of *Power Relationships*. The wisdom in these laws is founded on a purposeful yet selfless curiosity in our fellow man. Follow them and watch your fortunes improve. I will even share this book with my children as it holds many great lessons."

**—Steve Thomas, President, Global Sales, Experian**

"The easier it is to connect, the easier it is to communicate. It is what I remind our IGA Associates who serve the customers of our 6,000 stores throughout 21 countries. All of us at IGA thank Jerold Panas and Andrew Sobel for giving us 26 irrefutable laws in their newest book, *Power Relationships*. It will be an immense help in enabling us to blend and collaborate with our millions of shoppers."

**—Thomas S. Haggai, Chairman, IGA Associates**

"I was hooked after reading the first couple of chapters—what a neat book! *Power Relationships* provides amazing insight presented through engaging stories. I see our best people at ZS Associates applying some of the relationship laws in the book. Our firm can clearly benefit from these practical ideas, as can anyone responsible for clients and customers."

**—Jaideep Bajaj, Chairman, ZS Associates**

"Don't be confused. *Power Relationships* isn't about power. It's about building relationships that will stand the test of time. This book is solid advice for all aspects of all our lives."

**—Dick DeVos, President, The Windquest Group and Former CEO Amway**

"Mark Twain said it first: 'Common sense is indeed an uncommon quality.' Andrew and Jerry say it throughout *Power Relationships* in ways that put context and guiderails around social interactions. Like all great life coaches, these seasoned authors prepare us for life's journey, be it leaving for college as teens or traipsing the globe as corporate warriors. Buy the book. There is much to be gained from such a small investment."

**—Daniel M. Cain, Founder and Chair, Cain Brothers, LLC**

"It takes a life fully lived to write about power relationships. Andrew Sobel and Jerold Panas have each lived that life experience. They understand that real power is life giving. It's about meeting people where they are; listening to them; affirming their gifts and then calling them forth. *Power Relationships* is written for those of us who want to live life more fully; who are willing to risk and be vulnerable; who discover that it is in our sharing together of life experiences that we find meaning and wholeness."

**—The Right Reverend Frank S. Cerveny, IV Bishop of Florida**

"*Power Relationships* is a must read. It doesn't matter if the reader is not in a firm or engaged in business. It's for everyone. Andrew and Jerry's message and useful suggestions are inspiring and character building. Their approach makes their material fun to read. Each short chapter contains a parable based on a real-life experience. Varied and rich personal anecdotes provide lessons which may come as a surprise, at least to those who view power as a means to wield leverage over an adversary. Power in this book has another meaning. It is a means to achieve a goal. I am going to recommend this book to everyone I come in contact with—to executives, to leaders, to aspiring professionals, to everybody."

**—Francisco Gill Díaz, Secretary of Finance under President Vincente Fox and Regional Chairman of Telefónica for Mexico & Central America**

"I am delighted that Jerry and Andrew have dug deep into the study of human relationships, putting them at the forefront, both in business and at home. The 26 Laws for building Power Relationships describe some amazing ideas, from the first law about the importance of listening and holding great conversations to the last law on generosity and its dramatic effect. This book will transform organizations and individuals to be audacious, innovative, and persistent. It transforms principles of relationships into a program you can use in your everyday life."

**—Jaime Santibáñez Andonegui, CEO IMPULSA/Junior Achievement Worldwide**

# POWER
## RELATIONSHIPS

### 26 Irrefutable Laws
for Building
Extraordinary Relationships

ANDREW
**SOBEL**

JEROLD
**PANAS**

WILEY

Cover image: power icon © iStockphoto.com/Zeffss1; background art © iStockphoto.com/ RomanOkopny

Cover design: Wiley

Copyright © 2014 by Andrew Sobel and Jerold Panas. All rights reserved.

Published by John Wiley & Sons, Inc., Hoboken, New Jersey.

Published simultaneously in Canada.

No part of this publication may be reproduced, stored in a retrieval system, or transmitted in any form or by any means, electronic, mechanical, photocopying, recording, scanning, or otherwise, except as permitted under Section 107 or 108 of the 1976 United States Copyright Act, without either the prior written permission of the Publisher, or authorization through payment of the appropriate per-copy fee to the Copyright Clearance Center, 222 Rosewood Drive, Danvers, MA 01923, (978) 750-8400, fax (978) 646-8600, or on the web at www.copyright.com. Requests to the Publisher for permission should be addressed to the Permissions Department, John Wiley & Sons, Inc., 111 River Street, Hoboken, NJ 07030, (201) 748-6011, fax (201) 748-6008, or online at www.wiley.com/go/permissions.

Limit of Liability/Disclaimer of Warranty: While the publisher and author have used their best efforts in preparing this book, they make no representations or warranties with the respect to the accuracy or completeness of the contents of this book and specifically disclaim any implied warranties of merchantability or fitness for a particular purpose. No warranty may be created or extended by sales representatives or written sales materials. The advice and strategies contained herein may not be suitable for your situation. You should consult with a professional where appropriate. Neither the publisher nor the author shall be liable for damages arising herefrom.

For general information about our other products and services, please contact our Customer Care Department within the United States at (800) 762-2974, outside the United States at (317) 572-3993 or fax (317) 572-4002.

Wiley publishes in a variety of print and electronic formats and by print-on-demand. Some material included with standard print versions of this book may not be included in e-books or in print-on-demand. If this book refers to media such as a CD or DVD that is not included in the version you purchased, you may download this material at http://booksupport.wiley.com. For more information about Wiley products, visit www.wiley.com.

*Library of Congress Cataloging-in-Publication Data*:

Sobel, Andrew, 1955-
Power relationships: 26 irrefutable laws for building extraordinary relationships/ Andrew Sobel and Jerold Panas.
    pages cm
    ISBN 978-1-118-58568-9 (cloth); 978-1-118-83096-3 (ebk); 978-1-118-83097-0 (ebk)
  1.  Customer relations. 2.  Consumers–Professional relationships. 3.  Interpersonal relations.  I. Panas, Jerold.  II. Title.
    HF5415.5.S6216 2014
    650.1'3–dc23

                                                              2013033121


Printed in the United States of America

10 9 8 7 6 5 4 3 2 1

*The relationships in one's life are not just important—they are everything. In our business, at home, and among friends, relationships touch our lives in wondrous ways. They are the threads that weave through the fabric of our entire being. This book is dedicated to all who wish to experience the thrill and magic of power relationships. May they bring you fulfillment and success.*

# Contents

# Download the Free Power Relationships Planning Guide

To help you harness the 26 Relationship Laws, we've prepared and in-depth *Power Relationships* Planning Guide. It's a comprehensive, free ebook with dozens of worksheets and checklists that will enable you to put the Relationship Laws to work in your daily life. Go to either one of our websites to download it immediately:

http://andrewsobel.com or http://panaslinzy.com.

# 1

# The Missing Ingredient

We're going to tell you about 26 irrefutable laws that will help you build power relationships. These are professional and personal relationships characterized by trust, loyalty, respect, and generosity. They enable you to thrive in your career and give you deep personal fulfillment.

Our power laws apply without exception. They pass the tests of experience and common sense. You ignore them at your own peril.

We developed these laws based on extensive research. We have conducted thousands of interviews with senior executives and other personal contacts about the ingredients of enduring professional relationships. We've held endless conversations with high-achieving individuals in business and in the nonprofit sector. The laws we describe in these chapters have been percolating through the more than 25 books that we've written over the last 30 years.

These laws will enable you to engage with others in a way you never thought possible. Create lasting friendships. Win at work and in your profession. Connect as never before.

Study the laws. Leverage them. Follow them. You'll get powerful results.

Let us introduce you to the First Relationship Law. The story is about our friend Bill Jenkins. One day he got a wake-up call that changed his life.

Bill is a partner at a prestigious professional firm. He's bright and personable and holds two science degrees from top universities. In the past, he had so-so relationships with his clients. Mostly mediocre, he tells us. But something changed.

Within two years Bill rose to become one of the top rainmakers in his organization. He accomplished this transformation because he dropped his old beliefs about how to connect with his clients. He began following a new set of *relationship laws*.

"I had a client in New York," Bill explains to us. "He was the regional CEO for a large multinational corporation. I would see him about three times a year. One day, when I'm leaving his office, his executive assistant, Deborah, pulls me aside. I've got my briefcase in one hand and a large Power-Point presentation in the other.

" 'You know,' Deborah begins, 'My boss really enjoys having a conversation with you. You ought to come more often.'

" 'Well, I'm delighted he enjoys our meetings,' I tell Deborah. 'I do come fairly regularly. And we really prepare for these sessions.' I nod towards the thick presentation deck I brought with me.

"Deborah looks around, to see if anyone else might be listening. 'Your competitors are coming more often,' she says, now in a lowered voice.

" 'Thanks for that information,' I tell her. 'But I do feel like we have a good relationship. And I bring him lots of first-class analysis.' I shake the slide presentation one more time to draw her attention to it.

"She now leans toward me, whispering. I feel like she's about to share an enormous secret. 'I must tell you, my boss has confessed to me that he views those PowerPoint slides as the price he has to pay to have a *good conversation* with you!'

"At this point, I am stunned. I start thinking about all those slides I've dragged into my client's office!"

"What happened next?" we ask Bill.

"I reflect long and hard about this encounter. And I begin to change how I interact with the CEO and his other executives. I start seeing him more often. Our meetings are more casual and personal—sometimes over lunch, occasionally for coffee in the early morning.

"I start learning much more about his agenda, including his personal goals and ambitions. Because I'm seeing him more often, I'm in the flow of his daily life and can add more value to his day-to-day challenges.

"I still prepare for our conversations, but I don't often bring the PowerPoint slides. I start offering more ideas about his overall business challenges and growth opportunities.

"And as I learn about additional issues his company faces, I'm able to introduce other colleagues and expand our work. The CEO begins to see my firm and me as contributing to his company's growth strategy, not just as a spare set of hands to do operational analyses. Our discussions become more wide-ranging. We both seem to find our time together more enjoyable.

"Within two years," Bill tells us, "this becomes one of the largest revenue-producing clients at my firm. And I never go back to my old style that was all facts and figures. Never. Facts and figures might be an important part of your work, but they don't take you to the highest level of relationship building."

"What was your biggest insight?" we ask him.

"This is what I realized that day: *You build strong relationships through great conversations, not one person showing the other how much they know.* Some of my beliefs about what my clients valued had been wrong."

Bill's experience reinforced something we've observed for many years. The underlying assumptions you have about what leads to a good relationship make a huge difference in your behavior. And some of your assumptions may be the wrong ones.

Follow the right laws, however, and you build a vital network. You develop deep connections with clients, colleagues, influencers, family, and friends. You create an abundance of *power relationships*. Bill Jenkins did, and so can you.

Bill gives us the First Law of Relationships for this book: *Power relationships are based on great conversations, not one person showing the other how much they know.*

## How to Put the First Law into Practice

*"Power relationships are based on great conversations, not one person showing the other how much they know."*

Restrain your urge to impress others. Improve your conversations and you'll grow your relationships. Use these five strategies:

1. *Evaluate your current conversations.* How many of them meet the criteria for being great? For example, do your conversations help you and the other person:
   - Reflect and sharpen your views?
   - Improve your understanding of a problem or challenge?
   - Learn more about each other?
   - Feel moved or fulfilled?
   - Leave the discussion energized and wanting more?
2. *Stop presenting or pitching to others.* Turn every presentation—be it to a client prospect or to your boss—into a true give and take. Pause every four or five minutes to ask questions, probe for understanding, and create dialogue.
3. *Start actually listening and responding.* Other people know you're listening when you ask thoughtful questions about what they just said. When you synthesize and affirm. When you share relevant examples. When you empathize.
4. *Bring passion and emotion into your conversations, not just facts and analysis.* Ask, "How did you feel about that?" as well as "What did you think?"
5. *Make sure you're talking about the right things.* Don't be afraid to ask someone, "From your perspective, what's the most important issue we should be talking about right now?"

# 2

# Be Audacious

"I would like to speak to Mr. Penney, please."

The next voice I hear is J.C. Penney's. It's James Cash Penney, one of the greatest merchants of the last century and founder, at the time, of the largest retail chain in the nation. I'm actually on the phone with him!

I'll tell you more about the phone call in a moment. First, let me explain what led up to it.

I am in my early 20s. The Chamber of Commerce in Alliance, Ohio, has put me in charge of their Annual Meeting. A pretty bold move on their part for entrusting someone so young with the task. As one of my responsibilities, I have to get a keynote speaker for the meeting.

The year before, the Chamber drew 600 guests to its Annual Meeting. Being a bit obsessive and wanting to make a good impression on community leaders, I'd like to attract 750 men and women. I know it will take a very well known name to get that kind of a crowd.

I've just finished reading a book written by J.C. Penney. I am transformed. I call Ed Ahrens, manager of the local Penney's store.

"Ed, do you think there would be any possibility of getting J.C. Penney to come to Alliance to speak at the Chamber's Annual Meeting? Would you be willing to call him?"

"No. Not a chance. No way. And don't ask me again to try to get him. I would be embarrassed to even make the call."

So I do what you would expect. I go ahead on my own. I make the call. And now you know about the phone call. Here's how the conversation went.

"Mr. Penney, I just finished reading your book, *Jottings from a Merchant's Daybook*. I was mesmerized. If I know anything about you, you would not take no for an answer before even asking. Am I right about that?"

"Absolutely!"

"That's what I thought. Mr. Penney, we are having an Annual Meeting of the Chamber of Commerce in Alliance, Ohio. You have a great store here on Main Street. We want you to be our speaker. You are our only choice. I'll turn out the entire town for you." My voice is confident, but my heart is racing.

"I'd love to come," he says. "When is it?"

I give him the date. He does come. And we do turn out the whole town. Well, nearly a thousand people.

The phone call, and then the Meeting, turned into a lasting relationship. One that changed my life. I'll tell you about that in a bit. But first, the lesson. Here is the Second Law of Relationships: *Be unafraid to ask.* That's what I did—and you can do it, too. Reaching out to the right person could change and enrich your life forever.

Back to the Annual Meeting. It was a huge success. After the Meeting, I had the 86-year-old wonder sign copies of his book. We sold nearly 200 books.

When we left the auditorium and parted, we said our goodbyes. His final words to me were: "I wish you were a Penney man." I suspect this is the highest possible praise coming from J.C. Penney. I didn't walk to my car—I floated.

From that time on, I maintained an ongoing relationship with Mr. Penney (always *Mr.* Penney). Every time I went to New York, we would have dinner. His wife was gone by then, and he seemed pleased to see me.

The relationship grew. He was the grandfather I never had. He loved telling me about his first store in Kemmerer, Wyoming—and how it grew into another. And another. He often talked about his mother. She was his greatest inspiration.

He never tired of giving me advice. His favorite was: "Work hard. Work as if your life depends on it. It does."

I believe Mr. Penney was 91 when I got a call from his housekeeper. "Mr. Penney fell against the glass in the shower yesterday morning. He's at the hospital. I think he would want me to tell you." And, of course, I go to see him.

It is a few years later before I go to see Mr. Penney again. He is failing. He doesn't speak. It's a moment I will never forget. I am sitting beside his hospital bed. Once in a while, he opens his eyes for a moment. I am certain he doesn't know who I am. I hold his hand, this man who has become my grandfather, my hero.

There is no recognition. I get ready to leave. Then I stop. It seems he is trying to tell me something. His lips are moving.

I bend close. I can barely hear him. I lean closer. He whispers.

"I wish you had been a Penney man."

Celebrity, wealth, and power can present a seemingly unbridgeable divide between you and someone you'd like to meet. Make the first move. And then, cultivate the relationship over many years. Invoke the Second Law: *Be unafraid to ask.*

## How to Put the Second Law into Practice

### *"Be unafraid to ask."*

Here are steps you can take to begin crossing relational distances that you thought were insurmountable:

1. With whom would you like to connect? A well-known entrepreneur? A thought leader in your field? A CEO? Be bold. Make a list.
2. Next to each name, write down *why* that individual might be willing to help you.
3. Just do it. Start contacting the names on your list. There are many ways of getting in touch. There are some CEOs who will immediately answer their email. Try the phone.
4. Social media offers new opportunities to connect with outstanding or famous people. You could start by following them on Twitter or on their blog, and leaving comments. Eventually, your name may become familiar to them—and then they may take your call or answer your email.
5. Don't give up just because you've been turned down. Successful people usually admire persistence. You might get a yes on the third try.
6. Don't go too far and pester or annoy people. If multiple attempts haven't worked, take a break!
7. If you connect, mention something that you know is important to the other person—perhaps something they wrote, or an accomplishment they are proud of.

# 3 | Where Were You?

If you ever have a legal problem, call Catherine. She's a lawyer's lawyer. Smart, experienced, and calm under fire. She's been in the trenches, and also looked down at the trenches from on high. She sees the big picture as well as the minute details of every legal issue.

But there's a problem. You and I probably couldn't afford Catherine. She's a senior partner with a large, international law firm. She's worth every penny she charges, but her billing rate is out of this world. You have to have very deep pockets to get her services. That pretty much narrows the field down to a handful of large corporations who are facing bet-the-business decisions.

Oh, there's one other thing. Before becoming a senior partner at her law firm, Catherine was the general counsel for one of the largest companies in the world. It's a powerful and important position. For most, it would be the crowning achievement of an extraordinary career. Because of this, Catherine has what they call "street cred"—that is, the credibility that only comes from having had to live by your wits in the rough-and-tumble real world of business.

I'm having breakfast with Catherine, and I decide to get some free counsel. Not about legal matters—about relationships.

"Catherine," I begin, "I'm curious. As a senior partner, you are trying to build relationships with in-house counsel at large companies and sell your legal services to them. But just a few years ago *you* were the general counsel. You hired lawyers and law firms all over the world." I pause. "So tell me—what it's like being on the other side of the desk?"

Catherine stops eating. She shifts her gaze away from her scrambled eggs to me. I think I see a hint of a smile.

"Before I got promoted, I was the deputy general counsel at my company. But even though it was a very important position, the outside law firms we worked with—and other types of consultants—always wanted to talk to my boss, the general counsel. They often tried to bypass me. They thought he made all the decisions, and they invested everything in their relationship with him. They treated me more like a gatekeeper."

I can see where this is going!

She continues: "On the day the announcement of my promotion to general counsel hit the newspapers, my office was flooded with calls from big law firms all over the country. They all wanted to talk to me. They coveted my business. All of a sudden I was very popular."

I've now deserted my French toast. I'm all ears.

"So do you know what I said to all those blue-chip law firm partners who called me that day? The ones who never bothered to build a relationship with me?" She pauses. You can hear a pin drop at our table. "I politely asked each one of them, '*Where were you five years ago?*'"

Bam!

Many professionals ask me, "How can I build more relationships with CEOs and other top executives?" The best answer is the Third Law of Relationships: *Follow the person, not the position.* Build relationships with smart, motivated, interesting, and ambitious people, even if they're not in an important job right now. Follow them throughout their careers.

You see, really important people—those who are at the top of their careers in any field—have brought their advisors along with them over many years. While it is not impossible to break into someone's inner circle after they have achieved great success, it's also not an easy task.

Just look at what U.S. presidents do. After they win the election, who do they put into key roles in their administration? Do they scour the land for smart and capable people they have never met? No! They draw on tightly knit networks of those they know and trust. They put the individuals who led their campaigns and advised them in other roles into the really important positions.

Whether you're 20 or 50, you know interesting people who are going places. Follow them, stay in touch with them, and cultivate your relationship with them over many years. The fruits will be enormous. Not only will they help your career, but—perhaps more importantly—you will have an indelible impact on their success as well.

Don't just focus on connecting with top executives or other successful people at the peak of their careers. Go for the bright ones on the rise.

Before you know it, you'll end up knowing a sprinkling of very important people in high positions. And when this happens, the relationship will be very different than if you are a latecomer. You will share history together. You'll be relaxed around each other. You will be treated like the old friend you are.

The Third Law of Relationships will ensure that you build power relationships today with tomorrow's powerful people: *Follow the person, not the position.*

## How to Put the Third Law into Practice

*"Follow the person, not the position."*

Don't wait! In 5 or 10 years your network-building task will be much more difficult.

- Make a list of 12 to 15 people you know who are not yet at the peak of their success or careers. Pick passionate, motivated, talented individuals.
- Ascertain what their top three to five goals and priorities are. Knowing these, decide how you can best add value in the relationship.
- Stay in touch with these individuals regularly over time. Here are some ways to add value while you stay in touch:
  1. **Ideas and content.** Send them ideas, suggestions, perspectives, articles, books, etc. that relate to one of their interests.
  2. **Connection.** You can add great value by connecting your key contacts to other people in your network.
  3. **Personal help.** Are they new in town, and do they need help navigating schools and doctors? Can you offer some career advice? How else can you help?
  4. **Fun.** Can you invite them to a meal, a sporting or cultural event, or something else that you would both enjoy?
- Organize your staying-in-touch activities. Put them in your calendar so that each month you are implementing two or three activities to connect to and support these individuals.

# 4 | The Greatest Gift

I met Walter Wellesley Smith only once.

I doubt that anybody but his mother called him Walter. He was known to the world as Red Smith. He is generally regarded as the most outstanding sportswriter in the history of journalism.

We met at his desk at the *New York Tribune*. There was an Underwood typewriter, a high pile of blank sheets, a jar of paste, and a few red-leaded pencils.

Being with Red Smith was one of the highlights of my life. But that's a story for another day. What I want to tell you about is the conversation we had. It's all about relationships.

When Red was in grade school in Green Bay, Wisconsin, Adelaide Breckenridge was his homeroom teacher. I'm going to let Red tell you the rest of this story as best as I can remember it.

"Miss Breckenridge was in charge of my homeroom. She also taught me fifth grade English. She was tough. She made me work very hard.

"I remember a number of occasions when she would say: 'Red, you're made of great stuff. You are not showing your full potential. You can do really outstanding things when you grow up. You need to work harder.'

"It seemed that every time she had an opportunity, she would tell me about what high expectations she had for me. She'd tell me I had the makings of a good writer.

"Then I went on to junior high. On my very first day, there was Miss Breckenridge talking to my new homeroom teacher. It was before classes started. She asked me to join them.

"She said to my homeroom teacher that she felt I had strong prospects as a student and particularly as a writer. She asked that the new homeroom teacher look after me. More than that, she told her she should keep after me and push me.

"Every once in a while I would get a note from Miss Breckenridge. She wanted to know how I was doing and whether I was working hard. Her notes were filled with encouragement.

"When I got to high school, believe it or not, on the very first day there was Miss Breckenridge. She greeted me before class started. Other than exchanging a few notes, I hadn't had contact with her since I left grade school, and my first day at junior high.

"She took me up to meet my new homeroom teacher. 'I want you to watch Red and make him work hard. He is going to be a great writer someday. I'm counting on him. Sometimes he doesn't work as hard as he should and at times, he's pretty casual about his writing. You keep after him.'

"By now, I'm a teenager. And you know what—I began developing a close relationship with Miss Breckenridge. I guess that's what growing up is all about. We would write a couple times a month and we were calling each other pretty regularly. I would ask about the kids in grade school and she would, of course, ask about my English classes and my writing.

"During my four years in high school, our relationship became closer and closer. We only saw each other maybe once a year. But we kept in pretty close contact. I began thinking of how much our friendship meant to me. Here was someone who seemed to really care.

"I'm ashamed to tell you that after high school, I completely lost track of Miss Breckenridge. I didn't write her and she didn't write me. But I kept up with my writing.

"After college, I got a job at several different newspapers as a journalist. I was doing my best writing. Then I got a job at the *Tribune*. That's about as good as it gets.

"Then, the most exciting thing happened to me. In 1976, I was awarded the Pulitzer Prize. What an honor. What an honor."

Then Red goes to his desk drawer. He pulls out an envelope. The return address is a nursing home in Green Bay. The letter is addressed to him in very shaky writing, obviously from someone quite old. "I got this a few days after the Pulitzer was announced," he told me.

Red shows me the note. This is what it says:

Dear Red:
I told you so.
—Adelaide Breckenridge

I look at the note in silence. I think of the line from the Beatles' song called "Two of Us": "You and I have memories, longer than the road that stretches out ahead."

It's hard to understand exactly how relationships can develop. And why. Often, a person will take you under their wing. They become a role model for you. A motivator. They help you reach your highest aspirations. Think about your own circle and the lives you touch. You can be a mentor. Someone who encourages. You can help someone reach their loftiest hopes and dreams.

A historian pointed out that some of history's most accomplished individuals were raised by devoted mothers who fiercely believed in them. He demonstrated, for example, that President Bill Clinton and General Douglas MacArthur came from such backgrounds, as did the philanthropist Andrew Carnegie. So did many others. Is that surprising?

But obviously, it's not only about mothers. Having someone who deeply believes in you is a rare and powerful asset.

There's a law that governs this. It's the Fourth Law of Relationships: *The greatest gift is to believe in someone.*

It's a precious and powerful thing to give someone encouragement and show them what they can accomplish. To tell them, "You will be great." To believe in them, through thick and thin.

You will be able to say: I told you so.

You can have a transformative effect on a friend, family member, or colleague by simply believing in them deeply, consistently, and without asking anything in return. The Fourth Law will guide you: *The greatest gift is to believe in someone.*

## How to Put the Fourth Law into Practice

*"The greatest gift is to believe in someone."*

When the young Beatles were performing at the Cavern Club in Liverpool in the early 1960s, they were unknown. Enter Brian Epstein, who ran a family furniture store. He had utterly no credentials to become the Beatles' manager. But they hired him, and he was instrumental in helping them rise to fame.

Do you know what was possibly his greatest contribution to the Beatles? His utter and total belief in their greatness, well before they were recognized by the broader public.

"They are going to be bigger than Elvis," he confidently told anyone who would listen. Epstein relentlessly promoted the group, eventually getting them a record deal. And they did become bigger than Elvis, ultimately selling over 1.4 billion records. The Beatles' innate talent was fundamental to their success, but Epstein's unwavering belief in the young John, Paul, George, and Ringo was absolutely essential to their early development.

Start telling others how you believe in them:

- Who could use your support? Who do you know who needs mentoring and caring—someone to believe in them? Perhaps a family member, or a colleague.
- Begin by telling the other person how much you believe in them.
- Be consistent in your belief. Express it often. Follow up. If the person falls down, don't criticize—just encourage them onwards: "I know you've got the ability, and you'll do better the next time."
- Don't stop believing!

# 5

# What's the Agenda?

Your starting point for building a power relationship is always the other person's *agenda*. An agenda encompasses someone's goals, but it's even broader.

To show how important this is, let me introduce you to Richard Major. Richard taught me a lesson I'll never forget about understanding agendas.

Richard is a senior executive at his company, where he's worked for 25 years. He manages the very largest client accounts. The whales. He is not just good at what he does, he's one of the best I've ever met. But don't take my word for it—check his stats. He ranks number one in his firm for revenue production. And has for years.

If you meet Richard, you may—at first blush—think he lacks some of the finer relationship skills. He doesn't relish

small talk, for example. He's exceptionally bright, but sometimes uses a lot of filler words when he talks (*um, you know*).
But don't be put off by that. He has an unrivaled instinct when
it comes to building relationships with his clients, and a keen
eye for spotting opportunities for them.

When I first met Richard, I was consulting with his
company on a revenue growth initiative.

We're sitting in a big conference room, and some corporate honcho at the head of the table is interrogating everyone about how much more growth they can squeeze out of
their client relationships. He asks each executive the same
questions:

> "What's your stretch revenue goal for this client?"
> "What additional services can you sell?"
> "What's keeping you from accomplishing your goal?"

When Honcho gets to Richard, however, he meets an
immovable object. "So, what's your revenue goal for the
TCR Corporation next year?" Honcho asks him.

Richard's terse response to the first question is, "I don't
have one. It will depend on what the client needs." His reply
to the second question is similar: "I don't know yet. We
follow the client's agenda." He adds, "It's all about serving
their agenda of critical priorities, needs, and goals."

"Okay, okay." Weary, Honcho moves on to more fruitful
hunting grounds. Although he doesn't really understand how
Richard works, he respects the numbers.

During the coffee break, Richard pulls me aside. "I meant
what I said. TCR wasn't even a client 10 years ago. And now
it's the second largest account in the firm—over $30 million a
year in revenue."

The next day, Richard and I are having lunch at a sandwich shop along South Wacker Drive in Chicago. It's just the two of us now. No corporate honcho—he's back at the head office interrogating more people about their revenue targets!

I ask Richard a simple question: "Why are you so successful with clients?" I want to know his secret.

Richard is usually pretty serious, but now he looks at me, exhales, and smiles. "Let me show you something." He sets down his Diet Coke and reaches for something in his pocket. It's a small, folded sheet of paper. It's wrinkled and creased. It has obviously been opened and refolded many times. Richard slowly unfolds it.

I can't quite see it from across the table, but it looks like a list of names with some scrawls next to each name. Some words have been crossed out, and new ones written in next to the crossed out sections. Different pens have obviously been used at different times.

"You see this piece of paper?" Richard asks me. He holds the sheet out toward me. "This is a list of the names of my top clients. Next to each name I have listed that executive's agenda—his or her most important priorities." He pauses. I feel as though every other diner in the restaurant has stopped eating and turned to look at us, waiting to hear Richard's secret.

"My job in life . . . is to *help each one of them accomplish their agenda.* Period. That's my singular focus."

Richard's story clearly illustrates how your relationship-building journey must start with the other person's agenda. Not yours. Theirs. Whether you're talking about a client, a colleague, your boss, or a friend, your first job is to understand that person's agenda. Do you know what is important to them—really important—right now? Only when you understand this will you clearly see how you can help them and add value to the relationship.

The other person's agenda—as long as it is consistent with your values and ethics—is your true north when it comes to building relationships. It's your starting point for adding value. So the Fifth Law of Relationships is: *Know the other person's agenda and help them accomplish it.*

## How to Put the Fifth Law into Practice

*"Know the other person's agenda and help them accomplish it."*

Here's how you can become a student of others' agendas:

- A person's agenda comprises their three to five most important priorities, needs, and goals.
- In your work sphere, you should distinguish between someone's business agenda and their personal agenda—for example, completing a major project on time versus adapting to living in a new city. Both are important to know about.
- Think about your most important relationships, at work and at home. List these individuals. Do you really understand each person's agenda? Can you think of at least one or two things that are truly important to them? Then ask yourself: How can I help?
- Make it a habit to ask people about their agenda. Understand what is going on in their world. Here are five examples of agenda discovery questions:
  1. "How will you and your area be evaluated at the end of the year?"
  2. "What are the major goals you're being asked to accomplish by your leadership?"
  3. "What additional capabilities do you need to put into place to support and grow your business?"
  4. "Which of your initiatives will you personally be most involved in?"
  5. "What are you working on this year that you're most excited about?"

# 6

# The Billionaire
# and the Minister

I want to tell you about a most curious alliance. It was between
John D. Rockefeller and a Baptist minister, Frederick Taylor
Gates.

An early introduction grew into a friendship. Then into
a binding relationship. Dr. Gates ended up investing
Rockefeller's vast funds and was his most trusted business
advisor. He also saved Rockefeller's life. This happened when
Gates introduced him to a whole new world of philanthropy.

This is the story of how this came about. Step back in
history for a moment. Roll back the years. John D. Rockefeller is in his early 50s. His body is wracked with ill health.

Rockefeller is examined by his doctor. The diagnosis is a
death toll. "Mr. Rockefeller," his doctor tells him, "your
body isn't functioning properly. The prognosis is not good.

I have grave doubts about your living beyond the next 12 months.

"Let's try something," the doctor suggests. "I'm going to put you on a regimen that is quite severe, a diet of only goat's milk and soda crackers. (It was a diet he maintained the rest of his life.) And, most important, I want you to begin to spend less time making money and more time giving it away."

Enter Frederick Taylor Gates.

It starts modestly, this new business of giving money away. The philanthropy. And the diet.

Rockefeller's health is slowly improving. Every day the wealthiest man in the world walks down the streets of New York with piles of dimes in his pockets. He gives them to children on his morning walks. This is the beginning.

"Next in importance to doing the right thing," a newspaper quotes him as saying, "is to let people know you are doing the right thing."

His philanthropy continues to grow and so does his health. He lives until he is 98. Rockefeller and Gates become inseparable. It is an unusual and amazing relationship. The shrewd, brilliant money machine and the godly, Baptist minister.

"I have trusted Dr. Gates with my life," Rockefeller says. "There is no man I have greater faith in than him. I make the money, he invests it, and then he shows me how to give it away."

The philanthropy continues to increase. There comes a time when Dr. Gates convinces Rockefeller to make a gift of $400,000 to fund a new university. That was 1889. This was a considerable gift in those years. One day, Rockefeller summons Gates. "All right, I will give you $400,000," he tells him. "But there is one condition: I challenge you to get the leaders of Chicago to give an additional $400,000."

Gates does indeed raise the money. And then some. Rockefeller tells Gates that he is surprised he was able to raise that much money. He asks how Gates did it.

"It was not difficult. If you find a prospect big with gift, do not rush him too eagerly to the birth. Let him take his time with general encouragement. Make him feel he is making the gift, not that it is being taken from him with violence.

"Let him talk freely, especially in the earlier part of the interview. If your man is talkative, let him talk, talk, talk. Give your fish line and listen with the deepest of interest to every syllable."

This early money made possible the founding of a great university. It is known today as the University of Chicago.

Through the years, the relationship between Rockefeller and Gates becomes stronger. The bond grows closer. The two are constant companions. It gets to the point where Rockefeller begins using Gates for most business decisions and even family decisions. All of this in addition to the philanthropy. Gates becomes advisor, also, to the Rockefeller children.

This relationship is extraordinary. It is all the more amazing because Rockefeller almost never lets anyone get close to him. During his lifetime, he becomes the richest man in modern history. Also the loneliest. Except for his relationship with Gates.

The unusual but powerful and productive relationship between John D. Rockefeller and Frederick Taylor Gates is a case in point for the Sixth Law of Relationships: *Stretch yourself by building relationships with people quite different than you.* It was the very incongruity of the Rockefeller-Gates relationship, and the differences between them, that made it so productive.

Research shows that our natural tendency is to choose others to work with who are very similar to us. But the most creative teams, the teams that solve problems the fastest, are eclectic and combine people with very different backgrounds and personalities.

Look at the two founders of Apple, Steve Jobs and Steve Wozniak. Wozniak was a nerdy engineer who worked for HP. He single-handedly designed the hardware, circuit board, and software for the Apple 1 computer. Jobs was the mercurial, creative marketing genius.

He came up with the idea to sell the Apple 1 as an assembled circuit board—a complete microcomputer as opposed to a bunch of parts that hobbyists would assemble themselves. When Jobs's marketing brilliance, design flair, and showmanship were joined with Wozniak's extraordinary technical skills, the result was one of the greatest new companies of the 20th century.

Seek relationships in which there are differences between you and the other person. Possibly even, wide gaps in viewpoints, habits, characteristics. The divergence can create a healthy tension, an explosion of ideas, a change from the status quo.

Relationships with people who are just like you are easier. You can quickly agree on most everything. We gravitate toward those relationships. But that can be a problem. A certain amount of stress and tension is important. If you want to rise above yourself, put in the hard work it takes to accommodate differences. You'll be handsomely rewarded.

Truly life-changing relationships are often formed with the most unlikely individuals. Let the Sixth Law of Relationships guide you: *Stretch yourself by building relationships with people quite different than you.*

## How to Put the Sixth Law into Practice

*"Stretch yourself by building relationships with people quite different than you."*

We are drawn toward the customer or colleague who is friendly and likes us. It's often the difficult person, however, from whom we learn the most.

- Review your most important relationships, both professional and personal. Have you developed some with individuals who are quite *different* than you are? Have they stretched you? List them. Why have they worked for you?
- On the other hand, can you think of any relationships in which the whole is actually *less* than the sum of the parts? Why is this so? Are they "convenient" relationships that make no demands on you?
- Based on your first list, who is or could be your own Fredrick Taylor Gates or Steve Wozniak? List a couple of people, at work or in your personal life, whom you may not be naturally drawn to but who could push you and raise your game.
- Examine your own hot buttons or pet peeves that you have with other people. What sets you off? What kinds of people "drive you crazy"? List these qualities on a sheet of paper. Could these be preventing you from getting to know interesting people who could enrich your life and your career—and vice versa?

# 7 | Beware of a Cart Pulling a Horse

It's six in the evening, and I'm about to wrap up for the day. Then the phone rings. It's late. I'm tempted to let the caller leave a message. But I'm curious. I pick up the receiver and answer.

The other voice is animated. "Hello, I'm Sal Esposito. You don't know me." A pause. Then, "Wow, I can't believe I actually got you on the phone. And you answered it yourself!"

Okay, I'm not that famous. But I guess a little flattery won't hurt.

"Well, you caught me," I reply, "and I'm glad you did. I'm in between business trips."

"I'm such a fan of your books. Actually, all of us are here at Brown Stevens."

"I'm delighted you've enjoyed them. Which one have you read?"

There's silence as Sal thinks. "I really liked the one . . . the rainmaking one . . . you know, I think it was . . . maybe that one about the 10 strategies?"

"Ah, you mean *All for One*. I'm glad it's been helpful. Terrific." Sometimes people just don't remember titles. Or, they read someone else's book and think I wrote it.

"How can I be of help to you?"

Sal's enthusiasm is over the top—he sounds like a kid who just walked into his living room on Christmas morning and sees the tree with all the presents stacked under it.

"Let me explain. We've got a big push here to boost revenue this year. We think we have a huge opportunity to add new clients and grow some existing ones. We're leaving a lot on the table. The approach you take in your books really resonates with us here. It's just what we need. And we want to get started soon. Very soon."

I ask Sal a few questions, and he elaborates on what they're trying to do.

Most calls like this are exploratory. Usually, a potential client is just thinking about doing something. They feel dissatisfaction with their current progress, and want to explore getting help. Not Sal—he's champing at the bit. His company wants to start immediately!

*Wow*, I think to myself. This is the kind of call that you wish you would get once a week but that comes along only rarely. It's the blind date that turns out to be the man or woman of your dreams.

"We're ready to pull the trigger on this. Everyone's lined up behind it. What's your availability like? How soon could you start on a program with us? And how much would you charge? I know it's hard to say without getting more details, but maybe you could just give me an idea of your fees?"

Sal is so excited he can't contain himself. He's compressing what might normally be hours of conversations with a potential client into 20 minutes. We agree that I will send him a short outline with some ideas, and then we'll talk again in a few days.

Before I do anything else, however, I go down my checklist. Is this an urgent issue for the client? Yes. Does Sal "own" the problem—is he the right executive to be dealing with? He seems to be. Are they dissatisfied with the current rate of progress? Absolutely! Do they trust me as the preferred provider to help them? Well, they loved my books—it seems like they do.

Yet, something nags at me. I just can't put my finger on it. Sure, they had read one of my books and looked at my website. But they don't really know me. Still . . . I'm starting to catch Sal's excitement.

Over the next week, Sal calls me two more times. I finally send him a proposal, with several options. I still have a nagging feeling that something isn't quite right. But I brush it off—I'm ready to buy my plane tickets to fly out to Chicago where his firm is based.

We are due to talk the following week, but Sal cancels the call. Then, nothing. He stops answering my phone calls and emails. No signed proposal comes back. No kickoff meeting is scheduled. No conference call with his colleagues takes place as promised. The intensity of the deadening silence matches Sal's initial, unbridled enthusiasm. I've been proposed to and we've sent the invitations out to the guests. But now the groom has disappeared.

Three weeks later I get an email from Sal. It's short: "Look, I think we have to put this on the back burner for now. Some other priorities have emerged that we have to deal with. I'll be back in touch. We really do feel there's a great fit here. We just love your work."

That was five years ago, and I never heard back from Sal. Not once.

During my career I've had many encounters with others like Sal. The storyline is the same each time: The prospective client calls you and just can't wait to get started. And then, after you spend a week or two (or more) running around meeting their demands, the opportunity mysteriously dies. You are offered no more than a vague, curt explanation. Sometimes not even that.

Although I never did business with Sal's company, I can thank him and his "can't wait to get going—goodbye forever" friends for the Seventh Law of Relationships. There are actually two versions of this Law. The narrow version, which applies to sales, is this: *The eagerness of the prospect on the first call is often inversely proportional to the probability they will actually buy something from you.* Notice that I said "often." It isn't always true—but it is true often enough that you need to be aware of it.

The second version of this law is broader and more profound. It applies not just to sales but to many different endeavors in business and in life: *Serious engagement needs a relationship.*

I've learned there are no shortcuts when it comes to getting real and lasting results. You need the foundation of a relationship. In this case, I got taken in by the prospective client's enthusiasm and excitement.

Had I slowed things down, and built more of a relationship, there still might not have been a sale. But the odds of getting one would have been higher. I would have discovered what was really going on in Sal's organization. I might also have uncovered some red flags and not wasted my time.

I mistook enthusiasm for my books for a trusting relationship. But enthusiasm alone—for your products, your company's brand, or your personality—is not enough by itself to conclude a contract.

Before you win a sale—or gain commitment to anything important—you must build the foundation. The Seventh Law is short and easily remembered: *Serious engagement needs a relationship.*

## How to Put the Seventh Law into Practice

*"Serious engagement needs a relationship."*

If a commitment is happening too fast, it may be built on sand and quickly collapse. This is true of sales, but it's also true in other spheres.

Take politics: During the 2008 U.S. presidential campaign, Republican candidate John McCain chose then-Governor of Alaska Sarah Palin as his vice-presidential running mate. He barely knew her. He made the choice without spending any time with her. With no relationship between them, they campaigned completely separately, and presented a fragmented image for the Republican ticket.

Similarly, marriage counselors discourage short, precipitous engagements because they often see them resulting in divorce after only a few months or years.

Do you want serious engagement from someone? Ask yourself these five questions:

1. Have I taken the time to first build a basic relationship of trust?
2. Do I know enough about the other person or organization, and do they know enough about me, for this commitment to succeed and get off on the right foot?
3. Has the period of courtship been commensurate with the size and risk of the commitment?
4. Have I taken shortcuts in my normal process? For example, just because a friend recommended a job candidate doesn't mean you should abandon your standard hiring procedures.
5. What additional information do both sides need before I proceed?

# 8

## Found Guilty

C. Arnholt Smith.

I doubt the name means anything to you. At least not to most of you. But stay with me. This is a story about integrity. It was one of my most challenging experiences.

Smith was known by his friends as Arnie. I wasn't really in the "friends" category, even though I worked with him over a fairly long period. I called him Arnie as if he were a friend—and he didn't seem to mind.

He quit high school when he was fifteen and went to work in a grocery store. His financial success grew in monumental, unbelievable leaps. When the story I'm about to tell you takes place, he had the majority stock in the United States National Bank— the largest in California. He owned the San Diego Padres, and a dozen or so other major businesses.

He was an inspiration, the single most important leader in the community. The *San Diego Union-Tribune* named him

"Mr. San Diego of the Century." Among a number of other involvements, he was Chairman of the Republican Party and one of its largest contributors.

Come with me back in time to experience this story.

Smith is a strikingly handsome man. He is often seen riding around town in a tan Cadillac convertible. And he wears a tan suit to match, the very same color. No one can remember him ever wearing anything but the tan suit.

I had a fellow tell me once, who knows Arnie quite well, that he orders a dozen of these suits at a time, all tailor-made. And he has a suntan to match. I have known him for years and the tan is always there.

He is riding mountain high. Nothing could possibly go wrong. He is one of the wealthiest men in California, and among the top in the nation. He has a doting wife. A community that loves him.

Then suddenly, everything comes unraveled. Like the thread in a sweater you keep pulling on, and there is no end. It finally comes apart. A plunging fall from grace. I'll tell you more about that a little bit later in this story.

I'm advising on a major project in the city. I've helped them develop their fundraising strategy. The biggest possible coup would be to get C. Arnholt Smith as chairman of the campaign. His best friend, Malin Burnham, recruits him. Soon after, Smith makes a gift of $5 million to the campaign—a large gift now, but at the time, it was huge. In today's dollars, it would be around $25 million.

The campaign is several months old. But with Smith's gift, it's certain to be a success. And that reflects very well on me as the campaign's architect. Today, we're having a meeting of the Campaign Executive Committee. Lunch is over. The dishes are cleared. The meeting is about to begin.

Malin says, "Before you get to the campaign agenda, I have something terribly distasteful to tell you." That certainly gets everyone's attention.

"I'm going to report something no one else knows. And I can't tell you how I found out. You must keep it a secret. I need your pledge.

"In a month, the news will break. It will be all over, in San Diego, the state, and even nationally." Everyone agrees they will not break faith with Malin. They will not even talk about it at home. Whatever this is all about.

There is an edgy silence. Malin continues.

"I just found out that Arnie is going to be indicted for financial mismanagement. He will lose everything. The chances are very likely he will go to jail. The authorities found fraud, comingling of corporate funds, the siphoning of nearly $10 million from the bank, and income tax delinquency. And, possibly, illicit political donations."

Shock spreads throughout the room.

Malin adds: "We need to return his five-million-dollar gift. And of course, he can no longer be chair."

It's a punch to my gut. With Smith's donation, we could reach our goal. I am devastated. I want the money.

"Wait," I say. "Not so fast." I suggest a half-dozen different ways we could accept the funds. We can say it is a personal gift, not a corporate one. Or we could quickly use the funds until he was finally sentenced—you know, innocent until proven guilty. There were other ideas. Oh, I didn't want to lose the $5 million gift.

The pain is great. My stomach is churning. I feel queasy. All sorts of twitches.

But the committee is adamant. Integrity isn't important—it is everything. Malin says, "I'm the one who recruited Arnie and I'm the one who got the gift. I need to be the one to talk to him. I hope he will understand." Malin did, and that was that.

The fact is that the campaign was better off with no compromises. It was highly successful.

From that point on, Arnholt Smith plummeted into a purgatory from which he never escaped.

He was found guilty on all counts. Most thought that he would be sentenced to 10 to 25 years in prison. However, the judge (a very good friend of Smith's) received a medical report that Smith had only five years to live. The judge sentenced him to three years, saying, "I can't take those last two years of C. Arnholt Smith's life to keep him in jail."

There's not much more to report.

He was put in charge of tending the roses at the Federal Prison. His wife divorced him the day following the sentencing. His son died at the age of 36 of a heart attack. When he had served his sentence, penniless as most believed, he went to live with his daughter. He died at the age of 97.

C. Arnholt Smith's story illustrates the consequences of a lack of integrity. His. And it demonstrates the integrity of the group for which I was fundraising. It also highlights my temptation to rationalize when I think the goals are worthy. It reminds us of the Eighth Law of Relationships: *Integrity isn't important—it's everything.*

As for me, I've never forgotten the lesson. Someone once said the test for knowing right from wrong is whether you'd be willing to have your behavior in headlines in the front page of the newspaper the next day. (I was told that you are on the right track if you are willing to give your talking pet parrot to the town gossip).

Integrity is when you consistently adhere, through thick and thin, to a core set of irreproachable beliefs and principles. Your true north. In your relationships, integrity means honesty, consistency, and reliability.

Dishonesty and unpredictability are toxic. If you can't believe someone or depend on them, it's impossible to have a healthy relationship. You can't believe the message if you don't trust the messenger.

In the fifth century, St. Augustine wrote a now-famous book called *De Mendacio* ("On Lying"). He says, "When regard for the truth has been broken down or even slightly weakened, all things will remain doubtful."

After the Smith affair, I became a true believer. When I think back, I am embarrassed at my willingness to accept the $5 million. And frightened, also, to think I would be willing to compromise my principles for the money. Integrity is now the sine qua non in my life. It is not negotiable. It has become the mightiest weapon in my arsenal.

Tirelessly develop your reputation for integrity—for that state of honesty and wholeness. It becomes a powerful anchor for your relationships.

Each time you refuse to compromise your integrity, it gets stronger and more resilient. It takes years to build, but remember that you can lose it in an instant. Follow the Eighth Law: *Integrity isn't important—it's everything.*

## How to Put the Eighth Law into Practice

*"Integrity isn't important—it's everything."*

*You show integrity when you:*
- Are truthful.
- Follow through.
- Are consistent in your behavior.
- Are discreet and keep confidences.
- Uphold unchanging principles and values.
- Always keep promises and commitments, no matter how small.
- Walk your talk.
- Don't walk away from others' breaches of integrity.

*You risk losing your integrity when you:*
- Believe your goal is so important that you must do whatever it takes to accomplish it.
- Take small, seemingly harmless shortcuts. (Small lapses in integrity can lead quickly to larger, catastrophic ones.)
- Believe that sincerity absolves you from your lapses. (Remember: "All bad poetry is sincere.")
- Hold others to a higher standard than you yourself adhere to.
- Think "I'll do it just this one time . . ." or "Others are doing it. It's not so bad."
- Believe that because you are important, busy, and/or under pressure that doing something wrong is okay.
- Cross ethical boundaries in order to remain "competitive" in the marketplace.
- Add modifiers to your integrity ("reasonable integrity"). Something is either right or wrong.

# 9

# Never Steal a Bacon Sandwich

I'm sitting at the front of a large auditorium. I am the moderator for a panel discussion about trusted business advisors. To my left, seated behind a long table with individual microphones, are three senior executives. They were chosen because they have spent a lifetime selecting and hiring professional advisors and suppliers of all types.

The audience consists of the senior bankers from a prestigious global investment bank. There are more navy suits and red ties out there than I have seen since a large wedding I went to in New York. The audience wants to know about relationship building from the client's side of the desk.

I ask the first question of the panel. "Can you tell me about your most trusted advisors? Which bankers—and banks—are in your 'inner circle,' and why? What qualities do they bring to the table?"

The first CEO responds:

"The banker or any other person who is my trusted advisor is there for me through thick and thin. They aren't just present and providing advice when there are lots of fees being paid out. They come see me and add value even during the dry spells."

The other two executives nod with approval. Good answer!

The second CEO speaks:

"My trusted advisor always puts my interests first. He is willing to say no and push back. He asks thought-provoking questions and listens well. And, he has great integrity. He's utterly and completely reliable. If he tells me he'll have a report on my desk at 9 a.m. on Monday, it's there at 8 a.m. if not in my email inbox on Sunday night. And I never hear excuses."

More approving looks!

It's the third executive's turn. It's a zinger.

"At my company, we use investment bankers as little as possible. We avoid them. We have built up our own, in-house capability to do deals."

Eyes are wide open now.

"Can you tell us more about your approach and what's behind it?" I ask.

"It all goes back to something that happened 10 years ago. On a Monday morning."

"Ten years ago?" I interject.

"Yes, you see, corporations have long memories. At the time I was part of an internal mergers and acquisitions team that was assessing the possible acquisition of another company. We worked for weeks together on it, and things reached fever pitch over the weekend.

"We had literally camped out in a large conference room at our offices. By early Monday morning we had slept only about eight hours over the previous three days. Imagine the scene: We are unshaven and red-eyed. The room is a mess.

"At that point we need to appoint an investment bank. So we put one of the major banks we work with on standby over the weekend. The senior banker and his team agree to come in just before noon.

"In the meantime, we are starving. We order bacon sandwiches to be brought in. One for each of the four of us. When they arrive you can smell the bacon aroma 20 feet away! Shortly after we get the sandwiches, the investment bankers arrive.

"The head banker walks into the conference room. He is impeccably dressed. The required navy chalk-stripe suit, pink shirt, rep tie. We, on the other hand, are disheveled and wearing wrinkled shirts. Two of us are in our stocking feet. He spies the tray of bacon sandwiches on the table. A single sandwich remains because one of my colleagues has not yet eaten his."

The entire auditorium goes utterly silent. The crowd leans forward in their chairs, at rapt attention.

"The senior banker looks at the tray. 'Bacon sandwiches! I just love these.' He reaches for the last sandwich. My colleague is too polite to say anything. So the banker takes it and begins eating it enthusiastically. 'Mmmm . . . thanks.' Tomatoes and mayonnaise fly everywhere.

"My colleague's jaw drops. He hasn't eaten for hours and is dying to bite into his salty, greasy, delicious bacon sandwich."

There's silence. Some audience members are looking at their feet. I'm the moderator, but all I can say is, "Huh. And then?"

"Well," the CEO continues, "that colleague of mine, whose sandwich was taken, is now our Chief Financial Officer." Heads are shaking across the auditorium.

"We've never used that particular investment bank again. Never. Ever. They are still shut out, a decade later. And as I said, from that day on we began building up our own internal capability.

"So my advice to you is this: Don't eat your client's bacon sandwich if you want to become a trusted advisor."

Pockets of nervous laughter break out in the auditorium. The behavior the CEO describes is simply cringe-worthy. The man in the story had unwittingly reinforced and fed every stereotype and bias that corporate executives have about investment bankers ("They collect rich fees and then eat your lunch.").

Our friend the banker could have avoided 10 years in the wilderness if he had done a very simple exercise: to imagine what it's like to walk in his client's shoes.

So close your eyes and envision a different scenario. The banker arrives Monday morning. He knows full well that the client's corporate finance team has been burning the midnight oil for days. He knows they'll be haggard and sleep-deprived. In this imaginary version of the story, he's also sensitive to the fact that some clients feel investment bankers are a little full of themselves. So he'll be sure to go out of his way to be polite and respectful.

He walks in with a box full of fresh croissants from a local bakery and several steaming cappuccinos. He greets them, "How's it going?" Then he tells them, "I know you guys have been up half the night. Maybe these will help you keep going!"

Ridiculous, you say. Delivering coffee is not the job of high-powered bankers.

But think about it: By walking in his client's shoes, and acting on that insight, the banker would have utterly disarmed the client. Evaporated their biases. And the banker would potentially be picking up multi-million-dollar fees, year after year.

"Have some fresh croissants." You can imagine the stunned looks on the faces of the unshaven clients. The smiles.

He might have also said, later, "As soon as you called last night, we got together and started reviewing the scenarios you sent. We've got a few thoughts already about a third option. Let us know when you want to jump in." The message is: *This is all about you, and we're rolling up our sleeves and getting down to work as fast as we can.*

When we can only walk in our own shoes, we risk being full of ourselves. We repel others rather than attract them.

Which brings us to the Ninth Law of Relationships: *Walk in the other person's shoes.*

Our friend the banker didn't follow this law. Instead, he acted like an insensitive, self-absorbed blockhead. He lost millions of dollars in business.

Think about the pressures the other person is under. Imagine what they're feeling right now. Empathize with them. Become the person. You'll come across as engaging, trustworthy, and interested in their success.

As the famous country-western songwriter Joe South wrote, "Walk a mile in my shoes/Before you abuse, criticize and accuse/Walk a mile in my shoes."

It's easy to get wrapped up in yourself. To be blind to what others have been through and how they're feeling. Improve your empathy by following the Ninth Law: *Walk in the other person's shoes.*

## How to Put the Ninth Law into Practice

*"Walk in the other person's shoes."*

Here are nine practices that will help you walk in the other person's shoes. Follow these, and you'll be more empathetic, winsome, and engaging.

Think about the person you're about to meet with:

1. Picture the circumstances. What's happening, right now, in the other person's life? What pressures are they under?
2. Reflect on what you can do to make that person comfortable and relaxed.
3. Imagine what they are thinking. What's on their mind?
4. Imagine what they are feeling. What emotions are they experiencing right now? What will their mood be?
5. Lead with thoughtful questions about both thoughts and feelings.
6. Start with their agenda, not yours. Don't be so anxious to persuade and convince—to push your point of view on them as soon as you're together.
7. Think about how your ideas or proposals will be received. How will the other person react?
8. Try to help others come up with the right answer or best conclusion, as opposed to giving it to them directly.
9. Ask yourself how pure your own motives are. Whose best interests are you pushing? Is there a self-interest motive that you're pursuing?

# 10

## Oops!

He hated being president. I refer to A. Bartlett Giamatti. He was president of Yale University for 10 years.

Giamatti was a true scholar. That's all he cared about. But he knew that being president of a great university meant soliciting wealthy alumni for gifts. That's the part of the job he detested the most.

One of the people he is to call on is Fay Vincent. Vincent is a very wealthy alum. They are meeting for the first time.

Before the visit, the fundraising staff at Yale prepare the president for the meeting. For one thing, they tell the president that his father and Fay Vincent's father were classmates at Yale. They also give him a huge file of background information.

The president knows he has to call on Vincent. He dreads the visit. It is the worst part of Giamatti's job, but he understands how important it is. The appointment is made. I take you now to Fay Vincent's office. They sit around a small conference table in an office lined with books. Sipping coffee. Giamatti finally screws up his courage.

"Fay, I know you love the Law School at Yale. I'd like to talk with you this morning about making a substantial gift to the Law School."

Fay Vincent lets him go on for four or five minutes. Then he stops him. "Before you came down here from New Haven today, Bart, did you do some research on me?"

"Well . . . well, certainly. Of course."

"I assume there was someone from your research department at the university who did a little paper on me?"

"Actually, it isn't a little paper. It is quite a big file."

"Well, I'd fire that person."

"You would? You would fire the person? Why?"

"Because I don't give a damn for Yale Law School."

"You don't? You don't care for Yale Law?"

"Not a single warm cockle in my heart for Yale Law School." Long pause. A Quaker silence.

"Well . . . that's helpful information!" replies Giamatti.

"My father, on the other hand, was, as you know, Class of '31 at Yale College. He was captain of his football and baseball teams. My father loved Yale. And I loved my father."

Giamatti is still trying to recover. Finally, he says, "I know you loved your father, Fay."

"I'll tell you what I would have done if I were you, Bart. I would have taken all that research you did on me and thrown it away. I would have come in this morning and said, 'Mr. Vincent, I'd like to talk with you this morning about making a substantial gift to Yale College. We'll use it for financial aid, in honor of your father, the great athlete whom you love so dearly.' "

With that, Giamatti springs up from his chair.

He gathers all his papers and the proposal that are scattered on the table. In a moment, everything is thrown into his briefcase. He leaves without saying a word. Not a word. He closes the door quickly.

About thirty seconds pass. Then there is a loud knock on Fay Vincent's door. Vincent finally says, "Yes." He says it very slowly. Makes three syllables out of the word. Giamatti opens the door a crack. "The president of Yale is here this morning to talk to Mr. Vincent about a gift to Yale College. It will be in honor of his father, the great Yale athlete whom he loves so dearly."

"The president of Yale is now on the right track," Vincent says.

It was this first meeting that changed the life of both of these men. And it was a very personal connection—their fathers—that provided the catalyst.

It was an awkward beginning. But somehow, the awkwardness itself was a part of what drew them together. Things would never be the same for either.

They become as close as two brothers could possibly be. They find their mutual love of baseball turns out to be one of their most powerful bonds. Immediately following that visit, Vincent and Giamatti never miss a weekend together. They thoroughly enjoy each other's company. They somehow find time during the week to talk on the phone. They often have dinner together, and spend weekends with their wives in New York.

As for Giamatti, he wants to leave his job. He's tired of being president of Yale. All he wants in life is to become the

Major League Commissioner of Baseball. The baseball owners hear about this. They offer him the job.

It is a dream come true.

Shortly after he becomes commissioner, Giamatti establishes a new position in the League—that of deputy commissioner. He appoints his dear friend Fay Vincent to that job. Giamatti is in heaven. He loves his job. And he's working with his best friend.

But it does not end happily. In less than a year, Giamatti dies in office of a heart attack. Fay Vincent serves out the remainder of Giamatti's five-year contract.

There are times when two people meet and it is a difficult and stressful experience. There is awkwardness. Yet, when they discover a common love, a bond forms.

Have you ever known two people who have been happily married for many years, yet they had a difficult or even acrimonious start when they first met?

Don't be put off if you have a difficult start with someone. Awkward beginnings can launch wonderful relationships. Work at it. Find a personal connection that will draw you closer.

Take note of Bart Giamatti's and Fay Vincent's relationship. They were two very different people bonded by a common interest and a common history.

You may be a strong believer in first impressions. But withhold judgment. Follow the Tenth Law of Relationships: *Don't be put off by an awkward start—find something personal that connects you and you may develop a wonderful relationship.*

## How to Put the Tenth Law into Practice

*"Don't be put off by an awkward start—find something personal that connects you and you may develop a wonderful relationship."*

*The African Queen*, starring Humphrey Bogart and Katharine Hepburn, is a classic story about a wonderful, relationship that emerges from a bad start. In this film set at the beginning of World War I in German East Africa, Hepburn plays a Methodist missionary, Rose Sayer, whose village has been destroyed by the Germans.

She finds refuge with Charlie Allnut, played by Bogart, who pilots a small riverboat. Rose is snobbish and educated and has a strong moral code. Charlie is a hard-drinking, free-spirited, cynical boat captain who just wants to survive. At the beginning of the movie, they argue constantly and truly can't stand each other. By the end, however, they have slowly come to appreciate each other's strengths and share a mission to foil the Nazis.

In the finale, they are about to be executed by the Germans, and they ask to be married before they die. But they unexpectedly accomplish their mission of blowing up the German gunboat that has captured them, and they swim together to the shore—married and now free.

Here are four steps you should follow:

1. If you have an awkward start with someone, first ask yourself what you *liked* about the person.

*(continued)*

(*continued*)

2. Then, examine what is putting you off. For example, does the person:

- *Display a trait you dislike?* Ask yourself why that particular quality upsets you. It may not bother others, for example. Are you ever guilty of the same behavior?

- *Come from a very different background from you?* If so, you may not feel at ease with the person right away, but it could be an opportunity to learn more and expand your own horizons.

- *Seem uninterested in you as a person?* Sometimes we meet people and they don't pay us enough attention, so we perceive them as snobs or just uninterested in others. Is this a problem with your own need to be liked and noticed, or with the other person? Maybe they are just shy.

3. Actively seek commonalities. Ask lots of questions, and eventually you'll find a connection.

4. If you can find common ground, you can get a person to a higher ground.

# 11 | Don't Forget Your Wallet

It is a perfect evening. I still remember it vividly nearly twenty years later.

My wife and I are sitting at a table for two at one of the most talked-about restaurants in Paris. Our children are safely in the hands of a babysitter back at our hotel. You can just spy the Eiffel Tower out of one of the windows, lit up against a dark sky. The moon is nearly full. Romance is in the air.

The restaurant was just awarded a second Michelin star. The highest rating is three stars, and there are only a handful of establishments with that rating. A two-star restaurant, we had been told, is usually just as good as its three-star brethren, but half the price.

The meal is everything we expect. For an appetizer we both order sautéed langoustines with truffles. (Langoustines are those little pink lobsters, called *scampi* in Italy). For the main course, I have pan-roasted squab, and my wife has red wine–braised short ribs with winter vegetables. Oh, and the wine. The waiter recommended it—a delicious red Bordeaux.

The service is impeccable. Not too formal, not too familiar. We are in culinary heaven.

We stretch the evening out as much as possible. But all good things come to an end. As we linger over glasses of some kind of aged French Armagnac, I ask for the check. The waiter brings it. I discreetly pull my credit card out and place it on the tray on top of the check. Phew, it's a lot. But worth it.

The waiter comes back to pick up the check, and I immediately sense something is wrong. He has a very concerned, stern look on his face. He looks down at my credit card, his eyebrows arching slightly. "Je suis très desolé, monsieur." (Have you noticed that when something is said in French, it sounds special? Take, for instance, "savoir faire." The English translation, "know-how," just doesn't cut it.)

I understand—he's very sorry about something. What's going on? Why is he so sorry? He continues in English, "We only accept cash."

I am a deer in the headlights. The romance has abruptly ended. I scramble to pull out my wallet, but I know I don't have anywhere near enough money to pay for our extravaganza. I have about 100 francs in cash. That's enough to buy the mineral water we drank.

The waiter stands, patiently. We're at a standoff. "I'm sorry, we didn't know . . ." I imagine the Gendarmes arriving. I'll be like Jean Valjean from *Les Misérables*, imprisoned for years for stealing a loaf of bread (nothing compared to a whole dinner for two at this place!). I'm cringing with embarrassment.

Suddenly, a lifeline.

"What hotel are you staying at?" The waiter asks. We tell him. "Don't worry," he says, "I'll see if I can do something." Five minutes later he returns. "No problem, I spoke to your hotel and they are taking care of the bill." My wife and I exchange glances. We're astounded. And relieved.

The restaurant, and the hotel, trusted us. They assumed the best about our honesty and our intentions.

You might be thinking, "That was easy for them. The hotel basically guaranteed the bill." Not so fast: There was a leap of faith. Any number of things could have gone wrong for them in between letting us leave the restaurant without paying and getting their money.

Recently, I read about a similar incident at a steakhouse in New York City. An Italian tourist—a lawyer from Naples—ate dinner, then discovered he had left his credit card back at his hotel. He asked the waiter if he could go back to his hotel to retrieve it. He offered to leave his iPhone with the restaurant as a guarantee.

No dice! The restaurant called the police, who came and arrested the man. He spent the night in jail, only to be released by a judge the next morning.

The man and the police offer different versions of the story, so it's not totally clear what exactly happened. Maybe he really was trying to avoid paying for his meal. Or maybe, if the steakhouse staff had been willing to extend a little trust, they would not have ended up looking like jerks in every New York newspaper and the national evening news.

Our perfect evening in Paris could have also ended badly. But because the restaurant was prepared to trust us and our hotel, it had a happy ending. As a result, I've never ceased recommending both that restaurant and the hotel to everyone

I meet who is going to France. I have probably sent thousands of dollars of business to both of them.

We live in a low-trust world. Since World War II, our trust in just about everything—business, government, other people—has declined. And in many cases, it's declined for good reason.

But there's a vicious cycle that occurs: If you don't put any trust in the other person, they won't trust you. Which brings us to the Eleventh Law of Relationships: *Give trust to get trust.* There's a corollary law, which says that people become what you believe and expect of them.

If you believe your customers are all trying to beat you down on price and exploit you, then your own behavior will reflect and reinforce that lack of trust. You'll be stingy about sharing ideas and value in the sales process. You will inadvertently harden your customer's behavior. Your attitude of distrust will make it impossible to build a healthy relationship.

The same is true of your friends or loved ones. If you won't put trust in them, they won't trust you back—and worse, they will lose confidence in themselves. Distrust creates a vicious cycle.

In your dealings with others—at work and at home—assume at the outset that they have positive intentions. Be willing to start a chain reaction of trust. That will help you follow the Eleventh Law of Relationships and *give trust to get trust.*

## How to Put the Eleventh Law into Practice

*"Give trust to get trust."*

Here are five prudent ways you can build trust in your relationships:

1. *Assess the risk of trusting.* The higher the risk, the more difficult it is to trust. What's holding you back? What is the downside for you?
2. *Understand the essence of trust.* Trust is the feeling that the other person will honor your interests and meet your expectations of them. The specific elements of trust are:
   - *Competency:* You must believe the other person has the skills and experience to do the job they have promised to do.
   - *Integrity:* When you have integrity in the eyes of others, it means you're honest, reliable, and consistent.
   - *Agenda focus:* Before you trust someone, you want to know if they are simply focused on their own agenda or also on helping you achieve yours.
3. *Assume positive intentions in the other person.* Start by assuming the other person has positive intentions. Otherwise a downward spiral of distrust will begin immediately.
4. *Trust but verify.* You can give trust to gain trust while also making sure that others are earning your continued trust through their actions.
5. *Build trust through behavior, not words.* When you say, "Trust me!" it makes people reach for their wallets. Show you are trustworthy one step at a time.

# 12

# A Night in the Garbage Bin

On November 25, 2008, Citigroup executive James Bardrick stepped off his plane at the Mumbai airport in India. Waves of humid air washed over the crowd of debarking passengers. Bardrick slowly made his way through customs. At the time, he was co-head of Citigroup's banking business for Europe, the Middle East, and Africa.

He was 46 years old. His keen intellect, easy way with people, and fierce client devotion had propelled him rapidly up the corporate ladder at one of the world's largest banks. Square-jawed, youthful, and fit, he was affable and persuasive.

During his nearly 25-year banking career, Bardrick had experienced just about every professional challenge you can imagine. But nothing could have prepared him for the horrific nightmare into which he was to descend in less than 24 hours.

The next day, November 26, Bardrick met the CEO of a long-standing client. They were going to spend three days together, traveling around India to examine ways to expand the CEO's business there. He had a good relationship with his client, although today it is much stronger.

This is what happened next.

"Hans and I are eating dinner with a local lawyer, Raj, at the Oberoi Hotel in downtown Mumbai," James tells me. "Hans has been my client for several years. We've helped his company, a large multinational, in many areas. We lend them money, and we act as his lead investment banker for acquisitions and capital markets.

"As we sip our coffee, we are talking about doing business in India as a multinational company. Suddenly, we hear gunshots from outside the restaurant, just up the stairwell. Bang, bang, bang.

"It's loud and it's real live gunfire. And there are also screams. My heart starts racing. Hans, Raj, and I look at each other. We're frozen in our seats. What do we do next?

"Then, the maitre d' screams, 'Stay where you are. Stay seated.' Some of the patrons who have started to stand immediately sit down. But there's more gunfire. And now there's shouting.

"It's getting closer. Someone is coming down the stairs. 'Let's go. We shouldn't stay.' We jump out of our chairs and race toward the back of the restaurant, through the kitchen doors. The gunshots and shouts become louder behind us as we run into the kitchen."

James and Hans didn't know it yet, but they had the misfortune of being in the middle of one of the most horrific terrorist attacks of recent record. On that day, 12 coordinated shooting and bombing attacks occurred across Mumbai, India. One hundred sixty-four people were killed, and 308 wounded.

James continues his story: "Later, we learn that the terrorists killed about six people in the bar right near the dining room where we were sitting.

"We run through the kitchen. There's total chaos. People are screaming and rushing to and fro, knocking plates of food to the ground. Hans, Raj, and I are determined to get as far away as possible from the gunfire. We push into the rear of the extensive kitchen.

"From the kitchen, the hotel staff lead us into a ballroom. Eventually, there are a hundred people in the room. We sit in almost total darkness listening to the ongoing shooting and then, twice, loud explosions that I guess are grenades. It is very tense. Despite everyone having phones, no one really seems to know what is happening.

"We're certain that the police, at any moment, will swarm in and deal with what we assume is an isolated incident—perhaps a couple of fanatical gunmen wanting to make a crazy political statement. We're waiting for the lights to come on and to be told it's all over. Instead, we continue to wait, trying to control our fear. The terrorists could burst into the room at any moment and kill all of us.

"We wait. And wait. There is sporadic gunfire around us, and periodic shouts. We are tired, hot, thirsty, and sweaty. But we don't dare go back into the main hotel areas. Finally, we learn that a major attack is in progress. The hotel has been taken over by armed terrorists. We are trapped. They haven't found us, but we are, effectively, hostages.

"At this point the hotel staff tells us we should escape through a fire door that leads to the street.

"We open the emergency exit door and quietly slip out onto the alleyway that runs behind the hotel. What we don't know, but soon find out, is that the police and anti-terrorist squads have set up a perimeter around the hotel. They are attacking the terrorists. Anyone leaving the hotel is in danger of being shot—by the police.

"We can hear the sound of gunshots from inside the hotel. And more explosions. We walk down the alleyway, hoping it will lead us away from the hotel. But my heartbeat doesn't slow—it's racing faster than ever.

"We all walk up the narrow street, thinking it will lead us to the safety of the police who have surrounded the entire block. But suddenly we hear gunfire from right in front of us. A jeep is careening down the alley toward us at high speed. Sparks are flying from the rear. It is filled with more terrorists. Later, we learn the police have shot out the rear tires of their car in an attempt to stop them.

"Now they are coming straight at us, firing their weapons. We turn and start to run in the opposite direction. We are running as fast as we can in our leather dress shoes. Shots are coming from the Jeep as it gets closer and closer to us.

"We spy a garbage storage area on the side of the street. It's used by the hotel for refuse.

" 'Look, over there!' I scream. 'We can hide there.' The car is getting closer. My lungs are burning. It's the most intense fear I have ever experienced. Hans, Raj, and I leap onto the sacks of garbage. We can hear more gunshots. We burrow under the bags to conceal ourselves.

"You cannot imagine the putrid stench. Dozens of loose bags of restaurant refuse. Rotten food. Stinking liquid at the bottom of the bin. Maybe rats, too. But who cares. We're alive. They haven't found us! The gunfire is growing more distant.

"Eventually, it's quiet outside. But we don't dare to move. We don't dare to leave the safety of our garbage bin. A half hour passes. Maybe an hour. Finally, my client, Hans, whispers to me: 'Well, I guess this is one evening out together we won't forget.'

"We finally emerge, safe, at dawn. Raj is able to lead us toward his sister's house in a nearby neighborhood. Our final obstacle is a pack of menacing, stray dogs that blocks our way. But it's a minor threat compared to what we have just faced.

"Raj's family has been waiting up for us. They give us water, coffee, and even whiskey. Then, a delicious Indian breakfast. It's a memory Hans and I still relish.

"Everyone who stayed behind in the hotel became a hostage. The terrorists killed thirty-six people at the Oberoi. The three of us barely escaped with our lives. By minutes."

I am stunned by the time James finishes his story. Speechless. "Well," I finally say, "what an experience you two went through together. How's your relationship now?"

"When you go through something like that . . ." James trails off now. "When that happens with someone—well, it changes everything. It creates a powerful bond."

James Bardrick's story gives us the Twelfth Law of Relationships: *Change the environment and you'll deepen the relationship.*

Hopefully you do not have to experience this law in the way that James and Hans did. But the principle that was at work in the garbage bin in Mumbai works just as well in other, more pleasant locations.

Think about your own relationships. What do you experience when you go somewhere different with someone and are in a new environment together? Perhaps you bring a client to a conference in a city where neither of you live and you spend hours over dinner together. You get to know each other better. You talk about different things than you normally would. The relationship is intensified. Deepened. Stretched. Spending more time with your client in the office could never have the same impact.

Changing the environment will also deeply affect relationships with friends and family. My own family will never forget a nine-day river-rafting trip we took in Utah. It was arduous, with mosquitoes the size of hummingbirds. Scorpions. River snakes. Sizzling heat. Exhausting days. But today we still laugh about the trip. It bonded us. Brought us closer. It created a spectacular, communal memory.

Do something new and different with the most important people in your life. Get your client out of their office. Take your partner somewhere new. Doing so will activate the Twelfth Law of Relationships: *Change the environment and you'll deepen the relationship.*

## How to Put the Twelfth Law into Practice

*"Change the environment and you'll deepen the relationship."*

Social scientists have actually tested this law. They assembled two groups of couples that had been married for many years. All of the couples had a tradition of "date night": Each week they would go out to their favorite restaurant or a movie together. One group continued their practice and went to the same place each week.

The second group was told to vary their routine. Each week, they had to choose a different location and event. So they would go to the movies one week, a museum the next, dinner the next, and so on. At the end of the study, the couples in the group that had varied their date-night activity reported significantly higher levels of intimacy and feelings of affection for their partner.

The lesson for you: Change the environment.

Here are some steps you can take to leverage the Twelfth Law:

1. Get your clients into new "relationship environments." Invite them to a conference. Create an off-site event. Have them visit your company's offices.
2. Think about using your money to create experiences with the people closest to you rather than buying new things. Economists who study happiness have shown that money spent on experiences makes you happier than money spent on merchandise.
3. Be imaginative about creating new relationship experiences. Go on a vacation to somewhere you've never been before. Or take a vacation in your home city, spending each day exploring a new aspect of it.

# 13 | Don't Wait

"Who has been the greatest influence in your life?"

I wasn't prepared for that question. It's one I often ask other people when I want to probe deeply and get inside their heart and head. What's funny is that I have actually never been asked it myself.

Rosita looks at me, waiting expectantly. She's a journalist for the Mexican paper *Reforma*. After many years of working in Mexico with a wide variety of nonprofit organizations, the government has given me a citation for my contribution to the people of Mexico. It's from the Cabinet Minister in charge of Human Affairs.

I'm staring out at several hundred people in the audience who came for the award ceremony. I try to digest Rosita's question. A photographer is snapping pictures. There are microphones everywhere—radio and national television.

"So, tell me," Rosita asks in excellent English, "who has been the greatest influence in your life?" I actually have never given that a great deal of thought. But now I have to answer.

"It's my father," I tell her, almost blurting it out. I have never said that out loud before, and I certainly have never consciously realized it. He was the greatest influence of my life, and I didn't even know it at the time. My most important relationship.

Oh, the stories I could tell. He taught me to ride a bike. He never learned to do that himself.

There's another story I remember. I sat next to George Morrison in the fourth grade. He is the class bully. A huge guy. And I am the one he always picks on. One afternoon after school, he starts pushing me around. A large crowd gathers around us. We are fighting. I have never fought before. It's pretty bad. I come home with a broken nose and a black eye. My father says that we have some serious work to do.

He doesn't want me to fight, but he does want me to learn to protect myself. He teaches me how to hold up my hands, where to put my feet, how to duck.

Three months later, George is picking on me again. We're on the playground. He starts pushing me. We fight. This time, George goes home with a bloody nose and a black eye.

There's another time I remember. My father and I are walking on the beach. He asks me to pick up a handful of sand. He says, "Squeeze it as hard as you can." I do. And all of the sand runs out. There's nothing left.

Then he says, "Pick up a handful of sand and just hold it in the palm of your hand." All of the sand stays in place. "Life is like that. If you try to hold on to something too tightly, it escapes. Keep an open mind and an open heart."

There were bits and pieces of wisdom like that throughout my growing up. I could go on and on about the lessons I learned from him.

As I got older, I learned a lot about my dad. For instance, whenever we went out to dinner, he would tell me he forgot his glasses. He would ask me to read what was on the menu. The truth is, it really bothered me. I wondered why he simply couldn't remember to bring his glasses? I didn't find out until much later in life that he couldn't read English. He couldn't read in his native language, either. He left school in the third grade.

He taught me values and ethics. But it was always in parables—although he wouldn't have known what the word meant. Even now, as I write about it, the moments flash through my mind.

Later on, when he is too old to take care of himself, he is in a nursing home. I go to visit him. It is really no joy. I do it mostly out of duty. I watch him slowly fading away.

One day I get the call. He has passed away in his sleep.

It occurs to me, I have never told him how much he meant to me. Not once. I never told him how much I loved him. Not once.

I thought, as I'm thinking now as I write this, why did I wait? What is there about me that would not allow me to express what was in my heart? Even now, I'm punishing myself, "Lord, Lord, if you could give me just one more day with my father. Just one day."

The words I would tell him. The love I would express. I would let him know what a great influence he was in my life. I would tell him about all the important lessons I learned from him. I would let him know how much he means to me.

I am giving you the Thirteenth Law of Relationships so that you won't make the mistake I did: *Don't wait to let someone know how much they mean to you.*

Don't wait. Don't wait to let a person know how important they are to you. Don't let the opportunity pass you by.

Hurry up. For those you are close to, your family, friends, and mentors especially, don't wait to let them know how much the relationship means to you.

Don't wait.

As far as my father is concerned, I remember the words from that popular World War II song: "We'll meet again."

Think about the joy it would bring to those around you if they could hear directly from you about how much they have meant in your life. Follow the Thirteenth Law and start today: *Don't wait to let someone know how much they mean to you.*

## How to Put the Thirteenth Law into Practice

*"Don't wait to let someone know how much they mean to you."*

Think about how you'd feel if someone told you how much you've meant to them. Set off a chain reaction—tell others how special they've been for *you*.

1. Make a list of individuals who have touched your life in a special way. Start with just five names. Who has given you love and support? Who has been an important teacher? Who has inspired you?
2. Next to each name, write down why that person is important to you. List two or three things you have learned from them.
3. Now, go talk to each person on your list. Take them out to lunch. Write them a letter (not an email!). Call them on the phone. Get in touch in a personal way. You might start out like this: "I don't think I've ever said this to you, but I want you to know how important you've been in my life . . . there are a couple of really important things I've learned from you and I wanted to share them with you . . ."
4. Finally, encourage others to do the same. You could start that conversation by asking a colleague or friend, "Who's been important in your life?" And then, ask them, "Have you ever shared how you feel?"

# 14 | A Little Help for Your Friends

"I'm sitting in my parents' living room in Chatham, New Jersey. It's nine o'clock on a warm July evening. There's a knock on the door. Very strange for this time of night.

"You have to understand," my friend Steve explains to me, "Nobody just comes knocking on your door at night in Chatham. It's a small town and everyone goes to bed early.

"The loud knock takes me by surprise. I'm not even sure if I should go to the door and answer. My mother is at the beach. My father and I are in the back of the house watching a Yankees game.

"It's a very humid summer evening. I am working in New York City for the summer and have arrived home only twenty minutes earlier.

"I stand at our front door. Another knock. Finally, I open it. Standing in front of me is a young, African-American man in a blue Air Force uniform. He is standing erect and tall. His uniform is pressed to perfection. I am dumbfounded. I have never seen this young man before."

" 'Is Mr. Pfeiffer there, please?' I'm thinking: *Who is this person?*

" 'Mr. Pfeiffer? Do you mean Ben Pfeiffer?' That's my father.

" 'Yes. Mr. Ben Pfeiffer.'

" 'I'll get him. Please come in. Who shall I say is here?'

" 'My name is Clarence, I mean Clancy. Williams, sir.' "

Let me tell you about Steve Pfeiffer. He is recounting this story nearly 40 years after it happened. He has just stepped down as chairman of one of the largest law firms in the United States, Fulbright & Jaworski.

Elected three times by his partners, he served three terms as chairman over 10 years. Recently, after several years of careful study and open debate, his firm combined with Norton Rose to create a global legal giant. Nearly 100 percent of the Fulbright partners voted for the combination in a secret ballot election, a remarkable number representing a rare feat of consensus in a very individualistic profession.

Why was Steve Pfeiffer reelected so many times? It's called leadership. He's smart and has excellent judgment. He's also got humility and a deft, intuitive touch with people. He knows how to create followership—to get people aligned around a vision and a strategy.

That's Steve. And that's why I hate reading his resume. Way too many accomplishments: Commander in the U.S. Navy Reserve, Watson Fellowship out of Wesleyan, Rhodes Scholar, Yale Law School, Chairman of the Board of Trustees at Wesleyan, Council on Foreign Relations, law firm CEO, and more. Reading his achievements makes me feel like an insecure underachiever. And yet, unlike some very successful people, it's never gone to his head. He'll spend as much time chatting with the porter on the Amtrak train from Washington to New York as he will talking to the CEO at one of his client companies. Actually, he'll probably spend more time with the porter, especially if they're talking about the Yankees.

What happened that hot, humid evening in Chatham explains a lot about how Steve Pfeiffer became who he is today. And about the meaning of the Fourteenth Law of Relationships.

Now, back to the mysterious Clancy Williams. Steve continues the story.

"I yell into the kitchen for my father. He comes out, and a big smile breaks out on his face. He welcomes Clancy like a long-lost son. They talk animatedly about his Air Force career and how his mother is doing. I watch their interaction, and I'm puzzled. This young man doesn't just know my dad. He treats him almost as if he were his own father! There's an intimate quality to their interactions. Yet I had never heard his name mentioned in my family. They talk and hug, and after an hour or so Clancy Williams leaves.

"Later that night, I learn who Clarence Williams is. My father had an accounting practice in the next town over, Summit, where he had been president of the Rotary Club. Earlier he had been the mayor of Chatham. A woman who worked in the building where he had his office was a single mother. She was raising her children by herself. One of them was Clancy. She had very limited means.

"My dad helped her out from time to time, and took an interest in her children. When Clancy was a senior in high school, Mrs. Williams asked my father to speak with him about his future and about life. My father apparently told him he either had to go to college or enter the military to get some experience. Working at a low-wage job—or worse, just hanging out after high school and then getting into trouble—was not an option from my father's perspective. Clancy chose the military.

"As I got older I learned that my father often did things like this. He helped those around him whenever he could, in any way he could. He never publicized or talked about what he was doing. That's why I had never heard of Clancy Williams.

"I remember one Sunday morning when I was only about 10 years old. We were leaving church. I noticed a very shiny, brand new Cadillac go by. To my eyes it looked so luxurious. Inside was one of the members of our church and his family. 'Wow,' I said to my dad, 'Look at that new car they're driving! They must be doing really well.'

"My dad stopped on the sidewalk. He turned to me and in a stern tone said, 'You have no idea about that family or that car. When someone drives a car like that, you don't know if they borrowed the money to buy it, if they afforded it themselves, if they bought it but couldn't afford it—you don't know. Never, ever make judgments about other people based on their appearances. And never look up or down at anyone.'"

Reflecting for a moment about his father, Steve adds: "As a Christian I know the story of the good Samaritan from Luke Chapter 10 in the New Testament. After Jesus teaches his followers to 'love your neighbor as yourself,' a lawyer asks Him, 'Who is my neighbor?' Jesus answers by telling the story of the Samaritan who helps the injured man on the side of the road. My father didn't talk about this stuff, he just did it in his life."

As Steve tells me this story, the pieces fall into place.

Now I understand why Steve is as friendly and comfortable with the Amtrak porter as with a CEO of a large corporation. Why he has quietly mentored a small handful of young men from fatherless homes, helping with the cost of their education along the way. Why he used to host Wesleyan graduates from African nations at his house, some for weeks or months at a time, between semesters or until they could get settled in their careers. Why he recently helped a young girl from Sierra Leone get a visa and travel to the United States to be treated for horrific damage she suffered while undergoing a forced circumcision. Why he serves on the board of directors for Project HOPE, the NAACP Legal Defense and Educational Fund, the Africa-America Institute, and many others.

He sums it up for me in very simple words—giving us the Fourteenth Law of Relationships: "My father taught me that you should always be looking for ways to help the people around you. There's always something you can do, even if it's a very small thing. There's always someone around you who has a need."

"Great gifts mean great responsibilities." Whether at work or in your personal life, there will always be opportunities to follow the Fourteenth Law of Relationships: *There's always something, no matter how small, that you can do to help the people around you.*

## How to Put the Fourteenth Law into Practice

*"There's always something, no matter how small, that you can do to help the people around you."*

Researchers are continually searching for a scientific explanation for altruism. Early on, humans learned to practice what scientists call *reciprocal altruism*. Simply put, if you help others, they will remember it and help you. This practice helped social groups survive harsh conditions.

Another angle to this is Hamilton's Rule, developed by W.D. Hamilton. It states that our willingness to help or save someone else is a function of how *related* we are to them. So, you'd be more likely to rescue your drowning brother from a raging river than a second cousin or a stranger.

And finally, modern studies on happiness have shown that people feel better about their lives and are less depressed when they perform service to others.

These are interesting findings. But in the end, nothing can fully explain the desire to help others and the special satisfaction it creates in us. We all know, in our hearts, that it's the right thing to do.

So look for ways, big and small, to help those around you, like these three:

1. Do small things: Open a door, help someone put their luggage up in the overhead bin, give up your seat on a subway.
2. Every day, ask a loved one, friend, or colleague: Is there anything I can do to help you today?
3. Think about a bigger commitment to helping others. What could that be for you? What opportunities might you have to do that?

# 15 | Make It So

Mary Ellen Rodgers is a star. A superstar.

She is the corporate responsibility officer for Deloitte. Before that, she was managing partner for U.S. field operations. Deloitte is the second largest among the Big Four public accounting firms.

Mary Ellen is a member of the firm's exclusive Operating Committee. In 2012, she was named among the most influential women in the nation.

In her previous position, she headed the Western Michigan office in Grand Rapids. She was one of only three women in the firm's hundred-year history to head a major office. Often, the best man for a job is a woman!

This will give you an idea of Mary Ellen's effectiveness. As the head of a major office, she tripled revenue in just seven years. That should get your attention!

I'm sitting with her and talking about her work. I particularly want to know how she develops the client relationships that have managed to so greatly increase her revenue.

"Sometimes," she tells me, "it can take a long time to develop a relationship to its best. It takes persistence. At times, it's more a marathon than a sprint.

"There are no shortcuts to any place worth going. Often, a strong relationship is persistence meeting opportunity."

Then she tells me an amazing story.

It's all about patiently developing a very important relationship. It proves that unwavering determination can ignite glowing results.

"I worked for five years cultivating and developing a relationship with a huge potential client," she tells me. "Yes, five years! They had been using a competitor of ours for 40 years.

"I called, sent notes, and a few times simply showed up. I first built a small relationship with someone in the finance function. She then introduced me to the chief financial officer.

"From there, I found a way to connect with the chief executive officer. My first introduction to him was through a community event. Then, I creatively found ways to meet with him on a regular basis, month after month. Sometimes it was at his office. Other times I managed to see him at a firm event we had invited him to, a social event, or some other occasion.

"I never spoke to him about using our services, not once. I never talked about our expertise or our other clients. Never.

"Every time we met, I brought up new ideas. Innovation. Things that could be helpful in his business. That's what always got his attention.

"Our relationship grew over the years. I knew he was always pleased to see me. And I never had a problem getting an appointment with this busy CEO. Why? Because I always did my homework. I always had some interesting piece of information or a suggestion to share with him.

" 'Mary Ellen, what are you seeing in the marketplace?' he would ask me. He'd want to know how others were handling certain issues and challenges that he faced.

"One day, he calls me. 'Come and see me, Mary Ellen. This time, let's talk about Deloitte.' That was after five years. Five years!

"The relationship was very slow in developing. I let it take its course. Most people will tell you I move pretty fast, but I knew this would take time."

(It's true. Mary Ellen has only two speeds in her console. "Fast" and "faster.")

"It wasn't really about our expertise or our status in the industry. It was all about a trusting relationship with the CEO and always bringing him new ideas."

Mary Ellen's story illustrates a powerful relationship-building strategy: Act like the future relationship you desire *is already in place.* Mary Ellen treated a prospect as if he were already a valued client. And eventually he became one.

No one really wants to be sold to. That's why the best salespeople treat prospects like clients. They invest to get to know the prospect's business. They bring the executive new ideas and valuable market information.

This strategy works in other spheres as well. For example, one executive landed a top marketing position because he arrived at the final job interview with a twenty-page marketing plan to reposition the company's products. He acted like he already had the job. And he got it.

Want a great relationship with a friend or family member? Pretend you already have the loving relationship you aspire to. You'll be generous, kind, and patient—and that might just bring the other person along.

By the way, Mary Ellen's star continues to rise. Some predict she will be the first woman to head one of the Big Four.

> *Treat a prospect like a client, and there's a good chance they'll become one.* That's the Fifteenth Law of Relationships. Follow it and you may end up tripling your business, as Mary Ellen did.

## How to Put the Fifteenth Law into Practice

*"Treat a prospect like a client, and there's a good chance they'll become one."*

How do you treat one of your most valued clients? Read the following list, and think about how you could also do some or all of these things for an important prospect. Here's what you might do for an existing client:

1. Meet with them regularly.
2. Bring them ideas about how to improve their business.
3. Show them how other clients of yours are overcoming challenges similar to what they face.
4. Share valuable market information and insights about their competitors.
5. Make introductions to other relevant people in your network.
6. Invite them to events that your firm puts on.
7. Invite them to social or community events.
8. Orchestrate a visit to see another client's operations—an organization that has implemented a solution they are considering.
9. Ask them to participate in research you're conducting.
10. Invite them to speak at a conference you sponsor or participate in.
11. Recommend them for an industry or professional award.
12. Take an interest in their charitable or community efforts.

Why not treat a *prospect* this way?

# 16 | A Puppy Tale

It's September 23, 1952. The U.S. presidential election is only a few weeks away. Former General Dwight D. Eisenhower, the Republican nominee, has chosen a bright, up-and-coming young senator named Richard Nixon to be his vice-presidential running mate.

But a growing controversy is about to destroy Nixon's political career and remove him from the ticket. During the previous month, a furor has erupted over use of an $18,000 campaign fund. Nixon's opponents claim it was illegally used to pay for campaign and possibly personal expenses. It wasn't, in fact. In this case Nixon is innocent of the charges. His candidacy, however, is all but over.

You probably aren't going to like the protagonist in this story. You may even object to my using him in this book at all. And I don't blame you for feeling that way—when he became president, Nixon lied and committed crimes. But the lesson—the Relationship Law—is so powerful that I want you to remember it and use it. This example will make it hard to forget.

Back to Nixon.

Even Eisenhower, sensing the tide has turned against his running mate, is pressuring Nixon to quit. He sends word that Nixon should announce he is stepping down as candidate for vice president. It could very well be the end of Nixon's political career.

Nixon chooses instead a high-risk strategy: He decides to go directly to the American people on television and plead his case. He seeks to shift the court of opinion from the media to the people themselves. Sixty million Americans are watching or listening as he begins the speech of his life.

"I come before you tonight as a candidate for the vice presidency and as a man whose honesty and integrity has been questioned," he begins. He adds, "The best and only answer to a smear or to an honest misunderstanding of the facts is to tell the truth. And that's why I'm here tonight."

Nixon goes on to provide a great deal of information about his campaign finances. But he also shares intimate details about his life. Seven minutes into the 30-minute broadcast, he talks about his wife, Pat. The camera zooms out to show the whole set, and there is Pat Nixon. On the stage. She is sitting near her husband's desk, looking at him adoringly. This is unprecedented.

"I was born in 1913," he continues. "Our family was one of modest circumstances, and most of my early life was spent working in a store out in East Whittier. It was a grocery store. It's all the family had. The only reason we were able to make it go was because my mother and dad had five boys, and we all worked in the store.

"I worked my way through college and law school. And then, in 1940, probably the best thing that ever happened to me happened. I married Pat, who's sitting over here."

Someone had accused Nixon of using campaign money to buy a mink coat for his wife. So, after walking his listeners through his modest finances, Nixon says, "Pat and I have the satisfaction that every dime that we've got is honestly ours. I should also say this, that Pat doesn't have a mink coat. But she does have a respectable Republican cloth coat, and I always tell her she'd look good in anything."

Finally, the coup de grâce that solidifies the emotional resonance of Nixon's speech for those 60 million viewers: the gift of a Cocker Spaniel puppy, which they name Checkers.

Nixon admits his family got a gift from a political admirer. But it's not what most people are expecting to hear:

"We did get something, a gift. And our little girl Tricia, the six-year-old, named it 'Checkers.' And you know, the kids love the dog, and I just want to say this, right now, that regardless of what they say about it, we're gonna keep it."

Finally, he ends his speech with an act of extreme vulnerability. He turns his fate over to the viewers, saying, "Wire and write the Republican National Committee whether you think I should stay on [the ticket] or whether I should get off. And whatever their decision is, I will abide by it."

It's like he's kneeling over naked on the executioner's block, saying to the crowd, "You decide my future. I will abide by whatever you say."

The reaction to Nixon's emotional appeal is extraordinary and immediate. Enthusiastic crowds surge around him at the entrance to his hotel. Eventually, over four million cards, letters, and telegrams are sent in response to the speech. They run 75 to one in favor of Nixon remaining on the ticket with Eisenhower.

Historians say the speech cemented Nixon's support from middle Americans for the rest of his political career. With doubts about Nixon put to rest, he and Eisenhower swept the presidential election, and the Republicans took over the White House in January 1953.

Nixon's "Checkers" speech demonstrated the Sixteenth Law of Relationships: *Vulnerability is power.* When you are emotionally vulnerable, it allows people to connect with you. They root for you. They want to help you. It can create a powerful bond.

Some criticized Nixon's speech as contrived and even manipulative. But the vast majority of viewers saw sincerity and vulnerability. Nixon showed that he was an ordinary person—one of them. He laid everything out on the table for all to see. He threw himself at their mercy.

Emotional manipulation or authenticity? I've read several biographies of Nixon, and I've watched the video of the speech. I believe he was sincere. And so did most of the 60 million people watching the TV or listening to the radio that night. Nixon did lie later in his political career, but in the "Checkers" speech he told the truth.

As I said, you may object to my using Richard Nixon to illustrate the positive power of emotional vulnerability in relationships. This example might even infuriate you! But it was dramatic and powerful.

For better or for worse, those 30 minutes of very personal revelations changed the course of modern American history. Without it, Nixon's vice-presidential candidacy was dead in the water.

Modern research by psychologists has shown what Nixon understood intuitively: Emotional vulnerability fuels relationship intimacy. Whether you're a man or a woman, this idea may make you uneasy. Let me clarify.

Emotional vulnerability does not mean showing people how weak you are. It means sharing emotions and creating emotional resonance with the other person. It's about showing unvarnished honesty and disclosure. Admitting to a weakness may be part of that emotional resonance, but it's not the main thrust of it.

Here's some scientific evidence. One study asked a group of people to be measurably more truthful in their dealings with others. They were instructed to stop telling both major and minor lies. After 10 weeks of quantifiably greater honesty, they were assessed against a control group of individuals who had been given no special instructions.

When the study group members told three fewer lies per week than the control group participants, they experienced a variety of statistically significant health-related and emotional benefits. They began to perceive themselves as more honest people. Most important, the study authors report, "In weeks when participants told fewer lies, they reported that their close personal relationships had improved and that their social interactions overall had gone more smoothly."

People crave emotional intimacy and authenticity in their relationships. And they know when it's missing. For example, other studies have shown that when we tried to hide our feelings, the blood pressure of the people we're talking to rises.

But do we also value emotional vulnerability at work? Can it improve your professional relationships? Sure. Here's an example.

A large corporation told a client I advise that they would not renew a large, three-year contract. My client traveled to see them, and spent a whole morning—to no avail—trying to persuade the company to renew the contract. Most of the problem lay with the company itself. Nonetheless, they blamed my client for the breakdown in the relationship.

My client's chief operating officer went to his hotel that evening, overwhelmed with frustration. He wrote an email to the company that had pushed them aside. He reviewed the history of the relationship once more. He reiterated his commitment to addressing all of the issues that had been raised. At the end of the email, he wrote four simple words:

"Can we start over?"[*] He hesitated. Finally—and nervously—he hit "Send."

The next morning he had an email back from the company. "We've reconsidered. Yes, let's start over." They awarded my client a new, three-year contract that was larger than the first one.

Would they have gotten it anyway? I don't know, but my client believes that question—which made him vulnerable—is what tipped the scales in their favor.

> If you don't reveal yourself, your relationships will never reach the levels of trust and intimacy that are needed for deep friendship at home and partnership at work. Follow the Sixteenth Law of Relationships: *Vulnerability is power.*

---

[*] This particular question is featured in Chapter 8 of our book *Power Questions.*

## How to Put the Sixteenth Law into Practice

*"Vulnerability is power."*

The idea of being vulnerable is anathema to many. If you're a man, you may feel you're expected to be strong. Showing vulnerability is not what you signed up for. On the other hand, if you're a woman, you may be consciously trying to avoid the stereotype that woman are more emotional than men.

Being vulnerable doesn't have to mean collapsing in a heap or admitting to everyone around you that you feel inadequate. For example, all of the following 15 actions are very appropriate and productive ways of demonstrating emotional openness and the vulnerability that can accompany it:

1. Say you're sorry.
2. Admit you're wrong.
3. Empathize.
4. Ask for help.
5. Talk about how you feel—not just what you think—about an important issue.
6. Compliment someone.
7. Admit to a failure.
8. Ask for advice.
9. Use humor—joke about yourself.
10. Share problems.
11. Express heartfelt condolences if needed.
12. Share personal issues as appropriate.
13. Help someone else succeed.
14. Be honest.
15. Acknowledge others' contributions.

# 17 | The Carrot and the Stick

In his native Norway, he's better known than the prime minister of the country. When I walk with him down the street in Oslo, people line up to ask for his autograph.

The same is true in Amsterdam. In the Netherlands, where he now lives, they take their speed skating seriously. Very seriously.

I'm talking about Johann Olav Koss. It's been 10 years since he won his fourth gold medal in the Winter Olympics. That's some time ago, but Johann is still a national hero. A legend.

There's more. Johann also established three world records in the Olympics. In his skating career, he actually broke 10 world records. Many consider him the greatest speed skater in the history of the sport.

His achievements on the ice have been eclipsed by his efforts on behalf of an organization called Right to Play. This is an amazing international humanitarian movement founded by Johann. The work of Right to Play and the millions of lives of young people it touches every year is a story in itself. But not for now.

Let's get back to Johann and what turn out to be his two closest relationships. It begins when Johann is seven years old. He is with a large group of other young skaters. "I am the worst of the lot," he says. The leader and coach of this group of skaters is Svein Håvard Sletten.

"I am not very good. But Svein evidently sees something in me I don't see in myself. As I continue working with him, I realize he is a coach who wants most in life to produce a winner. That is my dream, also.

"He keeps pushing me. Pushing. Pushing. Hours and hours. Every day.

"But always, he only tells me everything I am doing wrong. I don't like all the fierce criticism. But that doesn't stop me from working hard. I work very hard. I keep improving.

"It's Svein's severe work ethic that drives me. It gives me the foundations to succeed.

"I keep driving myself. I work day and night at the skating. I am driven. I am totally committed to being the best. The best ever."

Talk about exerting himself. I once saw a video of Johann exercising when he was competing. It was a large stadium in Norway. There must have been a hundred steps in the stadium from the ground to the top row.

Picture this. There's Johann jumping with both feet together, one step at a time. Up all one hundred steps. If you don't believe that's tough, just try doing two or three steps, two feet at a time.

"Soon I am skating with a smaller group. Svein is still my coach. And I still get the negative comments. But now I'm with a more select group that shows real promise.

"I continue to improve. He continues to push me. But he never stops telling me everything wrong I'm doing with my skating. I'm not getting any positive strokes. Only what I need to improve."

Fast forward, as they say. Johann is now seventeen years old. He is discovered by Norway's National Olympic Committee as a very promising skater. They are always looking for the country's most promising. In Norway, skiing and skating are the nation's leading sports.

The National Committee wants to take Johann under their wing. They see something special in this young skater. But they want him to have a new coach, one of their coaches.

Johann makes one of the most difficult decisions in his young life. He accepts the decision of the National Committee to change coaches. After 10 years with Svein, he now has Hans Trygve Kristiansen as his trainer.

"What happens is that I am absolutely transformed. Instead of all the critical comments, my new coach is encouraging me. He's telling me all of the things I am doing right. Applauding.

"I start getting pats on the back instead of negative comments. It turns out the positive and reinforcing comments are the very thing I need. I am reborn. I begin to fly.

"Here's what's interesting," Johann tells me. "Both coaches were the greatest influences in my life. They had the most powerful impact. The relationships were abiding, but with a totally different imprint. One horribly humbling. The other, bolstering me with positive thoughts and encouragement. Hans had me reaching for the stars.

"These two coaches know each other, but they do not talk. They won't. But I maintain a close relationship with both. I care greatly about both, and they about me.

"I realize it is possible to maintain a very close relationship with two people, both of whom had a transformative impact on my life. Neither really likes the other—but they both care greatly about me."

Excellence is not driven by criticism or by praise alone. It requires a delicate blend, tailored for each individual. We know that to raise healthy children, parents must love them unequivocally. But parents must also give children truth—that is, tell them what they are doing wrong and push them to improve. To reach their highest aspirations.

In Johann's case, Svein's critiques early in his career helped create an extraordinary work ethic—an unstoppable drive. But later, he was lifted up to greatness by Hans's praise.

Johann Olav Koss's powerful experiences with his two dissimilar coaches gives us the Seventeenth Law of Relationships: *To reach their fullest potential, people need both truth and love.*

## How to Put the Seventeenth Law into Practice

*"To reach their fullest potential, people need both truth and love."*

There's no magic formula for the right mixture of truth and love. Sometimes a person needs unvarnished feedback, a tough critique of their performance, and firm direction. Sometimes they need praise, reinforcement, and unconditional support.

Here are five suggestions for implementing this law:

1. Assess your own style: Do you tend to find what's right or what's wrong with other people?
2. For many, it seems to come more naturally to catch people doing the wrong thing. Why not, as author Ken Blanchard suggests, walk around "catching people doing the right thing"?
3. Be thoughtful about what someone needs right now from you. Is it truth? Or love? Do they want and need to understand what they are doing wrong? Will encouragement be the best medicine right now?
4. Spouses beware: Researchers discovered that husbands and wives feel lower marital satisfaction when one is given *too much* advice from a spouse, as opposed to too little.
5. If you're going to confront someone with a fault or something they're doing wrong, you might first try and understand how they see it. You could start with a very general question like, "How do you see it?" or "What do you think is going on?"

# 18 | Draw Them In

I had never been to the Middle East before. It was no less sun-drenched and colorful than I had expected. A leading technology company had invited me to come and discuss a significant initiative they were about to launch. They had major operations in Tel Aviv, Israel, where I was to spend several days. It was a long trip to get there—7,500 miles—but I had high hopes.

I stayed at the Hilton, which is right on the seacoast. The rooftop restaurant has a breathtaking panorama. To the east, you look across the modern sprawl of Tel Aviv toward the West Bank. To the south, you gaze down the coastline and can spy small harbor towns like Jaffa. And out to the west, of course, is the sparkling Mediterranean.

The company I'm visiting wants to move away from a product and geographic focus to become a more customer-centric organization. I have the potential opportunity to help them design and implement this new approach. The plan is to spend a day interviewing various executives. Then, I am to meet in the early evening with the chief operating officer (COO) to try and seal the deal. If they are going to hire an outside advisor, the COO has to give his approval.

Here's the story. I have a very productive day at the company's offices. I learn quite a bit about the challenges facing the organization. In fact, I grow concerned about their ability to properly execute their plan. They face a number of risks in implementing their new approach. I'm a little worried.

At five o'clock my host brings me up to the 12th floor to meet with Aviv, the COO. I wait for 10 minutes. Then 30. What's wrong?

I wait some more. Then, a young woman comes into the waiting area and informs us that there's a problem. Aviv's schedule has changed and he only has five minutes to spend with me. Five minutes! 7,500 miles!

My host is crestfallen. "We can't go ahead without his agreement!" he whispers to me, as if the COO could hear us from all the way down the hallway. "This is terrible!"

I'm already running through different scenarios in my mind. How do I best use five minutes with the top dog? Should I ask him some thoughtful "power questions" about his plan? Reinforce my credentials by talking about my latest book? Share my conclusions from the day of interviews (but risk coming across as too forward)? Build my credibility by giving examples of recent client projects? Or, possibly, show that I am a peer and ask to reschedule the meeting when he has more time, perhaps the next morning?

Each of these approaches carries risks. I'm also reminded of the 7,500 miles.

One thing is for sure: I don't want him to feel that I am "pitching" him or trying to sell him my services. Instead of me leaning toward him, I want him leaning toward me.

"Mr. Barr will see you now," the young assistant chimes. Finally! I walk down the length of the corridor, and they seat me at a small conference table in the COO's spacious office. The large window looks northeast, toward the hills between Tel Aviv and Jerusalem.

Aviv comes in, obviously in a rush. He shakes my hand and sits down. "Nice to meet you. I'm sorry about the schedule change, but I can spare five minutes now."

I'm thinking. I look out the window to buy time. Then, back at Aviv. Suddenly, I have it! I've got a strategy.

"Aviv, we've only got five minutes. There are many things we could talk about, and questions I'd like to ask you. But since I was able to spend the day with your people, I wonder if the best use of our time wouldn't be to share my initial observations with you."

"Yes, yes, absolutely. Just give me your preliminary conclusions."

"You're planning a bold shift. It's a positive direction. But there are risks. Four, to be exact." Aviv narrows his eyes. I've got his full attention.

"Risks? No one has talked to me about risks. No one on my staff has articulated them. I want to hear this."

"First," I began, "When you make this transformation, there will be a loss of power among your executives who are currently responsible for geographic and product units. Some of them will drag their feet. They may even, subconsciously, sabotage the strategy."

Aviv is listening intently. His eyes are slowly widening.

"Second, if you're like many organizations, this initiative risks becoming the flavor of the month. You'll sound the trumpets, hold a big off-site meeting, and in six months another priority will emerge—I don't know, quality improvement or employee engagement. And you'll be on to the next big idea. Cynicism will set in. I see this all the time."

When we began, Aviv was leaning back in his chair—a posture of power—but now he is leaning forward, toward me. I go on to describe my third and fourth points—two further issues that need to be resolved before Aviv kicks off his program. And then I add a positive note and describe an opportunity that the current plan does not address. It's an interesting one that they have not thought of. Aviv smiles.

I quickly throw the ball into Aviv's court with a question about his reaction to the risks and the opportunity I described. Now we're in a conversation.

I end by saying, "There are ways you can mitigate or even eliminate each of these risks. Look, I know you've got to run, but I suggest that, if we decide to work together, we discuss these in greater depth at our next meeting."

My prospective client is on board. I have raised some issues with him that no one else has spoken about. Most important, I have *piqued his curiosity*. He wants to know more. He wants to delve deeper into the issues I have raised. He'd like to understand how the program could have an even greater impact. We shake hands and he runs off to his next crisis.

The next morning, before my alarm has even gone off, my host from the company calls me at the Hilton. He's ecstatic. "It went great. We got the go-ahead."

Oh, and guess how long the meeting lasted? We ended up spending 15 minutes together, not five. Fifteen minutes. You can cover a lot in 15 minutes. It's enough time to pass the sniff test.

The Eighteenth Law of Relationships helped me triple the length of the meeting and win a major project with this client. The law is this: *Make them curious.*

When someone is curious, they reach *toward* you. They want to learn more. They want to take the next step. When you evoke curiosity you create a gravitational pull that is irresistible. Curiosity helps you get more of everything: more inquiries, more sales, more clients, more dates if you are single, more RSVPs for your party, and more friends.

Create a powerful attractive force that draws others to you. In sales—and in life—always follow the Eighteenth Law of Relationships: *Make them curious.*

## How to Put the Eighteenth Law into Practice

*"Make them curious."*

Curiosity is *the desire to know*. There are many circumstances where it can be useful to evoke the other person's curiosity—to get them interested in learning more. These include sales, networking, and—yes—romance.

Here are some five rules for evoking curiosity:

1. Tell people what they need to know, not everything you know. Give brief answers to questions. Hint at things. Don't lecture a prospect for 10 minutes when they ask you to describe your firm.
2. Develop contrarian or unusual perspectives. Be seen as someone who has refreshing points of view.
3. Say the unexpected. For example, at the moment when people would expect you to brag about your accomplishments, tell them how lucky you've been and how ignorance may have actually helped your career at a key turning point. Surprise them by attributing a good part of your success to those around you.
4. Ask provocative questions. When everyone else is telling your client *how* to do something, you should be asking *why* they want to do it.
5. Tell people *what* you do and the results you get, not every detail about *how* you do it. The former is interesting; the latter can become tedious.

# 19

## Color Me Pink

It was one of the most exciting evenings I can remember.

I am in the 2,000-seat theater in the huge Dallas Convention Center. Every seat is taken. There must be another hundred people standing in the back.

As I look around, I see there are only a dozen or so men. The rest of the audience members are women. I'm at the Mary Kay Annual Seminar.

To get to the Convention Center, the taxi has to take me by the Center's parking lot. There are Pink Cadillacs as far as the eye can see. Hundreds and hundreds. An ocean of Pink Cadillacs. (Pink is Mary Kay Ash's favorite color. She awards her top 2,000 salespeople with a Pink Cadillac.)

I am involved in an important project for Mary Kay Ash. She thought I would enjoy attending the opening night of the seminar. It is an amazing extravaganza. An explosion of glitter and tinsel. A production that would have made Cecil B. DeMille pink with envy.

There is singing, a group of dancers, a pantomime performer, a juggler, a comedian (not so funny), a circus act. And on it goes. Forty minutes of show-stopping entertainment.

Then comes the moment. *The moment!*

The theater is totally hushed. Not a sound from the 2,000 audience members. Then the crowd breaks out in unison. "Mary Kay" (loud). "Mary Kay" (louder). And then, still louder: *"Mary Kay, Mary Kay!"*

The curtains part and out walks Mary Kay Ash. All five feet of her. All aglitter and aglow. The crowd is on its feet cheering. Screaming. It is pandemonium. Bedlam. Two thousand on their feet, cheering and clapping. The standing ovation must last a full five minutes.

Finally, Mary Kay walks to the microphone. There is 45 minutes of the most inspiring, motivating speech I have ever heard. She is interrupted every five minutes or so with a standing ovation and cheering. "If you think you can, you can." Cheering and clapping. "If you find a roadblock, take a detour." More cheering and clapping.

It goes on like that. I even find myself cheering. If someone had asked at the moment, I would have said, "Yes, sign me up. I want to become a Mary Kay representative."

A week or so later, I am back at her office building in Dallas. Mostly in pink, of course.

"Well, what do you think?" Mary Kay asks me. "How did you like the opening night?"

I am effusive in my praise. How could I not be? At one point, I ask how much an evening like that costs. (Wrong question!)

"I'd rather not think about it! But you have to keep reminding your top salespeople that you love them. There are two things people want most in life. They want them more than even sex or money. It's recognition and it's praise. We give them healthy doses of both."

In one short sentence, Mary Kay Ash gave us the Nineteenth Law of Relationships: *Show you care, often, by giving recognition and praise.*

A word about Mary Kay Ash. Then I want to get back to my story. There is more to come.

As far as Mary Kay's accomplishments are concerned, *Forbes* magazine named her Woman Entrepreneur of the Century. When she was in her mid-30s, she opened a small store in downtown Dallas. There was one salesperson—Mary Kay. During her life, the organization grew to nearly three million representatives all over the world. Almost all women. The corporation grew to $3 billion in sales.

It was my good fortune to be involved with Mary Kay for a period of more than three years. Every visit was always a lesson. There would always be a quote I would make note of.

I first thought of Mary Kay as the student, and I the highly regarded consultant—the teacher. But the student quickly became the teacher.

There were so many great moments. The most memorable experience I had, however, was when I was bringing my daughter home from college for Spring Break. We stop at a Marriott outside of Cleveland. We are sitting at a booth. We look at the menu and order breakfast.

Here's what happens next. The hostess ushers Mary Kay and her assistant to a booth right across from us. We greet. Hugs and kisses. I introduce her to Hillary.

"Do you mind, Jerry, if Hillary sits with me to have breakfast?" Her assistant joins me. Their conversation goes on for nearly two hours.

When we get into the car, I can't wait. "Okay, what did you guys talk about?"

Hillary tells me that it was mostly about women. "Mary Kay tells me that we have to work harder and longer than men in order to meet our goals. And if we don't have goals, we won't know where we are going.

"And she tells me that most of all, you want the other person to feel important. That's critical. Oh yes, you can achieve anything in life if you're willing to pay the price. And the price, she says, is to work very hard and be passionate about what you do. Mostly, Dad, it was women's stuff."

I kept in fairly regular contact with Mary Kay through letters and notes. When I was in Dallas, if her schedule permitted, I would have lunch with her in her pink office.

A year or two before she died, I visited her in her spacious home. Flowers everywhere. The truth is, she didn't look well. That vibrant, zestful woman was quiet and spoke barely above a whisper. I wondered if it would be our last meeting. It was.

I didn't stay too long. She didn't seem up to it or to want it. One of her parting remarks was something I'll never forget. "I don't know how much more time I have, Jerry. When I die, I want people to be able to say, 'She really cared.' "

That is what I would consider the most important characteristic of Mary Kay's life. She really cared. She didn't want any recognition. She often avoided it.

But she really cared about people. Whether it was the 2,000 top salespeople in her company, or the millions of representatives all over the world. Or breast cancer patients— her great passion. Or my daughter Hillary.

If it's not on her tombstone, it should be. If I had had any voice in the matter, I would have had engraved on her tombstone: *She Really Cared.*

Encourage those around you and bring out their best by following the Nineteenth Law of Relationships: *Show you care, often, by giving recognition and praise.*

## How to Put the Nineteenth Law into Practice

*"Show you care, often, by giving recognition and praise."*

What really motivates people? Is it money? Titles? The answer—which is supported by extensive research—is personal recognition for doing a good job.

Here are six strategies for recognizing and praising others:

1. *Praise immediately.* The more time that passes between the action and the recognition, the less impact you will have.
2. *Catch people doing things right.* Often, we look for mistakes. Instead, try watching out for positive actions.
3. *Praise the right things.* Don't praise a child for being a "champion" when they finished 18th in a race. Praise them for having the motivation to enter the race in the first place and for sticking with it to finish. Praise the wrong things, or over-praise, and your recognition becomes hollow.
4. *Be specific.* Don't just say "Nice job!" Describe exactly what you're praising the other person for.
5. *Make it personal.* A handwritten note is far more powerful than an email. A face-to-face expression of praise is more memorable than someone telling you second-hand that your boss's boss was happy with your performance.
6. *Don't mix criticism with praise.* If you praise someone, and then follow that with a suggestion for further improvement, you've just nullified the recognition!

# 20

# Are You Clever or Wise?

The auditorium is packed.

The company's top 200 executives have flown in from all over the world for their annual senior management retreat. That morning I have given a speech. I am invited to stay for another hour to hear the CEO's talk.

Standing at the podium, the CEO, Roger, concludes his overview of the company's strategic plan. "We have about 20 minutes left. I'd be happy to take questions and have some discussion." After a pause, a few hands go up.

"Roger, can you go back to that slide on last year's profit and loss statement?" one of the seated executives asks. "Did the expenses shown reflect any of the cost-cutting that took place at the end of the year?"

Another question follows: "Can you say more about the field reorganization that we implemented last spring? I'm not sure people fully understand it. I think there are still some lingering concerns about the way it was done."

Roger is having to review old decisions. He's being asked to parse the fine details of his financials. There's more: "Roger, can you go back over the decision to outsource our benefits management?"

The backward-looking, nitpicking questions go on for another 15 minutes. Roger keeps checking the clock on the wall. I can see his frustration steadily rise. I raise my hand. I don't know Roger very well—we've met only a few times. But I'd like to build a relationship with him.

"Yes? Do you have a question?"

I do. And it's an important one. I want to know what is really on Roger's mind. What motivates him. "As you look ahead to the next year or two in your business," I ask, "what are you personally most *excited* about?"

Roger looks up. He's been hunching his shoulders, but now he stands up straight, stretching his large, six-and-a-half-foot frame. He smiles, and takes a deep breath.

"Well," he begins. "Well, there is something." He describes an initiative that was not prominently featured in the formal plan. It's clearly the thing he is most enthusiastic about. The program he cares most about. He waxes on, now upbeat and energetic in his speech.

As we leave the auditorium, I walk with the crowd toward the door to the street. Suddenly I feel a large hand slap my back. Really—like a baseball mitt, whacking my shoulder. I turn around, ready to confront the perpetrator. It's Roger, the CEO. He's striding by me, heading out to jump in a car.

"Excellent question! *Thank you.*" He's now past me, heading to the exit. He looks back and adds: "That was a very revealing question." I am so surprised I can't manage anything more substantial than a smile and an "Oh, sure."

"Call me," are his final words as he hurries away.

And I do call him. And that is the beginning of an ongoing relationship with him and his company. The catalyst is a simple question that's little yet big. In an instant, it created three powerful shifts.

First, it shifted the conversation from a re-examination of the past to a conversation about the future.

Second, it took us from the details to the big picture.

And third, it moved us from the analytical to the emotional.

It's not that the past, the details, or the analytical are bad. Not at all. But right at that moment, the best question was the one I asked, which truly engaged Roger and drew him out.

That day, I wasn't particularly smart or clever. I didn't try to show off my expertise. I just asked a question.

My client's reaction illustrates the Twentieth Law of Relationships: *It's better to know the right questions than to have all the answers.* The 1988 winner of the Nobel Prize for Literature, Naguib Mahfouz, put it this way: "You can tell whether a man is clever by his answers. You can tell whether a man is wise by his questions." Answers are important. But if you want to create the great conversations that build power relationships, you need to become skilled at asking thought-provoking questions.

Thoughtful questions are essential to creating the vibrant conversations that fuel power relationships. A good question shifts the focus to the other person. It helps you understand their agenda. It ensures you're talking about the right issue to begin with. Good questions create deep personal knowledge and make the other person feel listened to.

Questions are to relationships what salt is to food—they bring out the flavor and intensify the richness.

Use thoughtful questions to engage others and focus the conversation on the most important issues. Follow the Twentieth Law of Relationships: *It's better to know the right questions than to have all the answers.*

## How to Put the Twentieth Law into Practice

*"It's better to know the right questions than to have all the answers."*

Be bolder with your questions. Think and plan ahead. Go to every meeting with a client or your boss with three thoughtful questions. Turn statements into questions. Think about using the types of questions we ask below. Note that most are open-ended—what, why, how:

1. Access emotions, not just analytical thought ("What are you most excited about right now?").
2. Draw out others' views ("What do *you* think?").
3. Engage the other person in the solution ("What options are you considering? What do you think is the best decision for you?").
4. Focus the conversation on the right issues ("What would you like to talk about? What's the most important thing we should discuss?").
5. Uncover the other person's agenda of key priorities ("What are the most important things you'll be evaluated on this year?").
6. Access the other person's highest-level goals and aspirations ("Why do you want to do that?").
7. Challenge ("Do you think that's enough? Is 10 percent high enough?").
8. Help establish your own credibility ("Many of my clients are grappling with two big issues right now. . . . What has been your reaction?").
9. Explore who the other person is and how they became who they are ("How did you get your start?").
10. Restart the conversation when it's gotten off on the wrong foot ("Do you mind if we start over?").

# 21

## For the Sheer Joy of It

In Oswego, Kansas, people are mighty proud of their twelve-bed community hospital.

There are other hospitals in larger neighboring cities. But people in Oswego wouldn't think of going anywhere for their health care other than their local hospital.

One person told me, "We get here whatever you can get at Mayo. Except the staff is friendlier here." Well, that may be a stretch. But that's how folks in Oswego feel about their hospital.

Mary Jane Cummins is the Development Director at the hospital. That means she raises money for the hospital. She splits her time between that and admitting patients.

The Development Office is in the basement of the hospital, in a corner tucked away in a long corridor. You need to really want to get to Mary Jane's office in order to make the trip.

Mary Jane doesn't have any training in raising funds. But she's passionate about the hospital and totally dedicated. That outstrips experience every time.

For over a decade, Sam Anderson comes by her office every year. It's usually in October. He calls ahead to make certain Mary Jane will be around.

It's obvious they have a strong relationship. He likes her (everyone does). She likes him.

In he walks. Bib overalls and a plaid shirt. As far as Mary Jane can remember, it's the same bib overalls and plaid shirt all these years. She thinks it may be his dress-up to come to town from his farm.

"Mary Jane, here's my twenty-five dollars. I wish it could be more. I love the hospital. I hope this will help some." They hug and Sam leaves. He's been giving the same amount, twenty-five dollars, for all these years.

In December of each year, Mary Jane bakes bread for her "special people." Sam's gift is one of the smallest at the hospital, but to Mary Jane, she knows Sam stretches to make it. He is one of her special people.

Her visits with the bread are always a few days before Christmas. She travels all over Oswego to deliver the home-made bread. And usually last on the route is Sam's farmhouse.

Fast forward, as they say. This last year, Sam lost his soulmate. It was in August. He and Agnes had been married for 57 years. Sam didn't make his regular October visit with his gift. Mary Jane called him several times, but never said anything about the gift.

Now it's Christmas. Even though he didn't make a gift, Mary Jane bakes Sam a loaf of bread. She adds some cookies to the package. She drives out to the farm.

They talk for a long time. She holds his hand, tells him how desperately sorry she is about his losing Agnes.

Mary Jane is so pleased she has made the trip. She's heard Sam has become a recluse since Agnes died. He doesn't leave the house.

It's time to leave. She gives him the bread and cookies, along with a long hug. It has been a love-filled visit.

"Just a minute, Mary Jane, before you get ready to leave. I have something I've been planning to give you." He leaves for the bedroom.

Before continuing this story, I am going to give you the Relationship Law that explains the bond between Mary Jane and Sam. It's this: *A selfless motive creates powerful bonds.* It's when neither party is trying to gain something. A pure motivation is the most wonderful catalyst for building relationships.

Now back to my story. You remember that Mary Jane is ready to leave. Sam asks her to wait a moment.

He goes into his bedroom. In a few minutes, he comes out with two huge shopping bags. He staggers under the weight. He tells Mary Jane that he will help her carry the bags to the car.

"Agnes and I decided five or so years ago we were going to make a trip. In all our years, we have never been outside of Oswego—except for our honeymoon in Topeka.

"We started saving coins and some spare dollar bills whenever we could. We really scratched. There was never much left over. The last time I counted, there was over $2,000.

"A couple times a month, we would skip dinner. That way, we could throw a couple extra bucks into our getaway bag."

"I guess I'm not going to be able now to make that trip with Agnes. I'd like the money instead to go to the hospital."

They hug. Cry. And finally say goodbye. He shouts as the car passes by, "And thanks for the bread. Agnes always loved it."

It's inspiring to be in the presence of someone whose intentions are pure and who gives freely and selflessly. Remember the Twenty-First Law of Relationships: *A selfless motive creates powerful bonds.*

## How to Put the Twenty-First Law into Practice

*"A selfless motive creates powerful bonds."*

Few stories in literature so beautifully illustrate this law as O. Henry's short story "The Gift of the Magi."

It's Christmas, and Jim and his wife, Della, live in a modest flat. They have only $1.87 left. Della's prized possession is her waist-length, beautiful, flowing hair. Jim's beloved possession is his gold watch, handed down to him from his grandfather and father.

Della has no money to buy her husband a Christmas present, so she cuts her long hair, sells it for $20, and buys Jim a platinum fob chain for his gold watch.

Separately, Jim sells his beloved watch to buy Della some beautiful tortoise shell combs for her hair. They are the same combs she has coveted in the window of an expensive shop.

Christmas day arrives. Jim and Della discover that each has sold what they most treasured, in order to give something special to the other. O. Henry writes, referring to their unselfish motives, "Let it be said that of all who give gifts, these two were the wisest."

Whenever you give, test your own motives. Remember, a selfless gift works in magical ways:

- It can help an important charity or a nonprofit. (We give for many reasons, usually for the sheer joy of helping others.)
- You hold a light for others to see. You become a powerful example that encourages others.

*(continued)*

(*continued*)

- You can end up leaving an indelible imprint on someone's life.
- If you give out of pure intent—whether it's helping a colleague at work or someone who is down and out—it shapes and polishes your own character.

# 22

# A Tale of Two Cities

Meet Ellen and Peter. They are both partners with large, well-known public accounting firms. They both went to good schools. They each have years of experience in auditing the financial statements of Fortune 500 companies. Consummate professionals.

But that's where the similarity ends.

Ellen is a trusted advisor to the chief financial officer (CFO) of her largest client. Peter, in contrast, is tearing his hair out. His principal client has been trying to cut the fee for his firm's audit services. He struggles to even get on the CFO's calendar.

Let me describe a bit about each of them. You'll quickly understand the differences. And, you'll learn about one of the most fundamental laws of relationships. If you follow this law—if you master it—it has the power to utterly transform

133

your role with clients and customers. Actually, it will transform your relationships with most of the significant people in your professional life, including your boss and your colleagues.

Interested? Read on.

First, Peter.

"They're driving me crazy," Peter tells me over lunch. "This client sees the audit as a commodity. They just want the lowest price."

"What kind of relationship do you have with the CFO or his deputy?" I ask.

"Not much. They have basically delegated the management of the audit to their VP of finance, who reports to the CFO. He, in turn, has turned over the day-to-day relationship with us to their Director of Audit. I rarely see the CFO."

"How would you describe your role with your clients?"

Peter looks up at me like I'm a bit nuts. "My role? My job is to get the audit completed on time and on schedule, and with an unqualified opinion. That's what auditors do!"

As our lunch progresses, a portrait of Peter emerges. He is what I call an "expert for hire." The tip-off was the board dinner he once got invited to.

"A couple of years ago," Peter begins, "a client told me that his company's board of directors was interested in talking to me about some accounting and tax issues. I guess they felt they needed to educate themselves. They asked me to attend an informal board dinner. I was really excited about the opportunity."

"So what happened?"

"I got to the dinner, and as soon as we sat down the questions started. My host, unfortunately, hadn't been very specific about the issues the board members wanted to discuss."

"Oh?"

"The first question came out of left field—it had nothing to do with accounting: 'So how long do you think the Federal Reserve will continue its current low-interest rate policies?' I managed to stumble through an answer. Nothing brilliant. Then, the next one: 'How do you think China's accelerating investments in Africa are going to affect commodity prices?'

"I was," Peter admits with candor, "pretty clueless on that one. And most of the other questions that followed."

He adds, "And I thought they wanted to discuss the latest accounting regulations."

Peter is a great accountant. He knows his stuff—his accounting rules and methodologies. The problem is, most top executives don't actually care about that stuff—at least not the details. They want a job done, not a lecture on the regulations of the Financial Accounting Standards Board.

That's where Ellen comes in. I first met Ellen when I interviewed her as part of a panel at a client off-site conference. She is known to have an uncommon knack for building strong relationships with her clients at the most senior levels.

That day, I ask her what her secret is: "What makes you successful with clients?"

"It starts," Ellen tells the packed room, "with how you define your role with the client. My first responsibility is to achieve an unqualified audit opinion for my client, and to use all of our latest methodologies to help complete a successful audit.

But I feel my mission is also to be a business advisor to my client. I help them manage their financial assets productively and reduce their risks. I'm a sounding board for new policies and strategies. At the highest level, my job is to help my client achieve their growth and profitability goals."

"Can you say more about that?"

"Sure. When I take on a new audit client, I tell the chief financial officer—or, in a very large company, the deputy CFO or SVP—that I want to have a regularly scheduled lunch every two weeks.

"The reaction is the same every time: 'No way! I don't need to have lunch twice a month with my auditor.' But I insist. I tell them, 'I do this with all my large, significant clients. They find it a very valuable practice. It will help avoid problems and highlight opportunities early on.'"

"And what happens then?" I ask Ellen.

"After a couple of these lunches, my clients are hooked—they love the interaction. I use these as occasions to really learn about the CFO's priorities and goals. I share best practices from other clients.

"We discuss everything from strategy to that new opening they have for a controller, and how we could help by suggesting some candidates. I share issues we are seeing in their field operations. I provide intelligence about their organization that other advisors can't see because they are not close enough to the business.

"But the lunches are only part of the picture. Basically, all my exchanges with my clients are framed in the context of their big-picture goals—their growth, profitability, and innovation. I don't want them to see our audit as a necessary evil. Rather, I want them to see me as a strategic advisor who does a terrific job each year getting their audit done smoothly and without complications."

"How about fee pressure," I ask Ellen. "Do your clients try and get a discount from you?"

"Well, of course, in large companies there is always a drive toward getting the lowest fees. And they do try to negotiate.

But actually, I see the opposite occurring. My clients are often asking for us to do *more* work, not less. The more we demonstrate that we are helping to improve their business, the more frequently they reach out to us for additional services."

Ellen and Peter are real people. The dramatically different roles they play with their clients highlight the Twenty-Second Law of Relationships: *Become part of your clients' growth and profits and they'll never get enough of you.* The flip side of this Relationship Law is that if a client views you as an expense to be managed, they'll cut you at any time.

Think about it. If your plumber calls you up and suggests you have lunch to discuss the latest joint-soldering techniques, you probably would decline. And, as much as you like him, if another reputable plumber offered to do a major job for significantly less, you might very well be swayed to accept.

But what if your doctor called? "I've got your test results back, and you ought to come by so we can discuss them." I think your response would be, "How soon can you see me?"

Peter, to his clients, was a plumber. They didn't want to have lunch with him. Ellen's clients, in contrast, thought of her as a personal physician.

> If you can show how what you do directly supports your client's growth, you'll harness the power of the Twenty-Second Law of Relationships: *Become part of your clients' growth and profits and they'll never get enough of you.*

### How to Put the Twenty-Second Law into Practice

*"Become part of your clients' growth and profits and they'll never get enough of you."*

A client can replace a commodity "expert for hire" at any time—perhaps with a cheaper expert. But a provider who is seen as supporting a client's most essential programs is not easily replaceable. Their cost is framed against a much larger set of benefits.

This law doesn't just apply to client relationships. For example, if your boss views you as directly helping her achieve her most important goals for the year, then you'll be considered indispensible.

Follow these five practices to be seen as part of growth and profits:

1. Focus your proposals on what your client needs to have done, but also frame your work in terms of how it will help your client grow, innovate, and be more profitable.
2. Make sure you truly understand your client's agenda of critical priorities and goals. What are they trying to accomplish this year?
3. Gain an equal understanding of your client's personal agenda. What is the equivalent of "growth and profits" for them on a personal level?
4. Talk about your *value* with your client. Emphasize impact, not methodology, during the sales process.
5. Define yourself as in the business of improving your client's condition, not just doing a project or fulfilling an order.

# 23 | To Die For

The most famous personal transformation in history took place one day in AD 35. The events surrounding it are generally well accepted by historians of all stripes, religious and non-religious.

Saul, who was later known as Paul the Apostle, was a powerful leader in the Jewish religious establishment of ancient Israel. He was educated, affluent, and influential.

One day, however, he gave up his old life entirely. He dedicated himself to a person who appeared to him on the road to Damascus. It was Jesus of Nazareth, who had been executed several years earlier. The members of Paul's entourage also reported seeing a bright light and hearing a voice.

What makes the story even more extraordinary is that Paul was on his way to arrest some of Jesus's followers. Paul subsequently traveled thousands of miles by foot, horseback, and ship to spread the word about Jesus.

History tells us that for over twenty years Paul endured repeated beatings and stonings as he journeyed all over Asia Minor. He was flogged several times to within an inch of his life. He was jailed and kept in chains. He was shipwrecked three times and chased out of major cities by angry mobs. And finally, he was put to death in Rome for upsetting the authorities with his unflinching views.

Today, we talk about having "followers" on social media. It's a badge of honor. But Paul's followership was something else altogether. He possessed a dedication, a devotion, that was of a vastly different order of magnitude.

But he wasn't the only one. We read that Jesus, for whom Paul was such a dedicated exponent, originally had 12 disciples. What many don't know is that the majority of these disciples also died horrific deaths for Him. By preaching Jesus's gospel, they constantly put their lives at risk. And they would not recant their beliefs, even under torture and threats of painful execution.

Peter, who was the disciple closest to Jesus, was also killed in or near Rome.

James, son of Zebedee, was put to death by Herod Agrippa I shortly after Passover in AD 44.

Andrew was reportedly crucified in Turkey.

Matthew, according to legend, died a martyr in Ethiopia.

James, son of Aphaeus, was stoned and clubbed to death in Jerusalem.

Thomas was murdered with a lance in India. A large Christian community, dating back to his time there, thrives today.

They were all killed because they would not renounce their belief in their leader (for them, their Lord). It would have been easy to disavow Him and save their lives. But none of them did.

There are two remarkable facts about this story. First, that Jesus only needed 12 followers to start a worldwide movement. It was a movement that, within a few hundred years, overturned Roman political domination and polytheistic beliefs. And later grew to several billion adherents. The second remarkable thing is that these 12 disciples were so loyal to Jesus that they did not hesitate to die for Him.

What explains the apostles' extraordinary, life-altering followership? The short answer is that Jesus's disciples were willing to die for Him because *He was willing to die for them.* They trusted Him and believed in Him.

And why only 12? Jesus knew that 12 supporters such as these were more powerful than large crowds of fickle, fair-weather followers.

Shortly before His death, Jesus called his disciples together. He commanded them, "Love each other in the same way I have loved you." Then, alluding to his imminent betrayal and crucifixion, he said, "There is no greater love than to lay down one's life for one's friends."

Jesus had truly loved his disciples. He had taught them and trained them. He had infinite patience with them. He then took the punishment from the authorities for them.

Have you ever had a boss or colleague like that? Someone who mentored you, nurtured you, and stood by you? A boss who gave you the credit when things went well? And then took the blame when things went badly? (Usually it's the other way around!)

Whether you take Jesus's death and resurrection as actual history or metaphor, the subsequent writings of His disciples show that they saw His sacrifice as the ultimate proof of His leadership and His love for them. And they dedicated their lives to spreading His story and His teachings.

Twelve disciples. Twelve followers. How could so few have been so sufficient? They had no cell phones or Internet to spread the word. No force of arms. But through their unflagging devotion they won over other followers. Word of mouth spread like a wildfire.

This story has great relevance in an age when we have become obsessed with building up hundreds and thousands of friends and followers through social media. In a culture where we relish networking almost for its own sake.

Jesus and his 12 disciples illustrate the Twenty-Third Law of Relationships: *To succeed, you need a small group of people who trust you, believe in you, and are committed to you—not hundreds of superficial contacts.*

Who will go out of their way to endorse you and introduce you to their network? Who will drop what they are doing and help you when you are in need? Who will tell others that they've never known someone as trustworthy and talented as you? For these things, you need a handful of great relationships.

Do you know a small group of people who will walk through a wall for you? Perhaps more importantly, are *you* willing to put yourself on the line for them? Have you given them your unwavering loyalty?

Make sure you have loyalists, not just acquaintances. Follow the Twenty-Third Law of Relationships, which has been at work for thousands of years: *To succeed, you need a small group of people who trust you, believe in you, and are committed to you—not hundreds of superficial contacts.*

## How to Put the Twenty-Third Law into Practice

*"To succeed, you need a small group of people who trust you, believe in you, and are committed to you—not hundreds of superficial contacts."*

Sociologist Robin Dunbar theorizes that we can each maintain around 150 stable social relationships. This is now popularly known as "Dunbar's number."

But how many truly meaningful relationships does anyone really have? The hundreds of professionals we've interviewed say that if you really boil it down, they've had perhaps 12 to 15 essential relationships in their career.

Who would be on a list of your "critical few"? Look at the seven categories following. Can you think of important individuals you need to deepen your relationship with?

1. *Clients and customers*. If you work in business, these are the lifeblood of your career.
2. *Catalysts*. These are individuals who can introduce you to others and make a transaction happen.
3. *Colleagues*. Studies show that strong internal relationships provide a critical foundation for your success.
4. *Collaborators*. In your work, you may have other organizations or people that you collaborate with.
5. *Donors*. These are essential if you work in the nonprofit sector.
6. *Counselors*. Who is a mentor or advisor to you?
7. *Family and friends*.

# 24

## Start an Epidemic

Close your eyes for a moment.

Picture a boxcar. You know, the car from a freight train. With the sliding doors. Okay. Now think of that one freight car with sheets hanging from the ceiling to divide it into rooms.

That's how Mannie Jackson grew up. That's where he was born and lived through grade school. Even more remarkable, there were 12 family members who lived with Mannie in that freight car. Twelve!

This is a true story. It is far too remarkable to have been made up.

Mannie today is considered among the 30 highest net-worth African Americans in the country. And ranked among the most influential. He serves on a number of corporate boards.

His net worth is in the high millions and growing every year. He plans on giving away $100 million to charity.

It's a remarkable journey. *Boxcar to Boardrooms.* That is, by the way, the title of the book he wrote to describe his bold pilgrimage. It's a story worth telling. He didn't read a book until he was 12. There were no books in the segregated school he attended.

What he soon discovered was that he could jump. Boy, could he jump.

He could jump higher than anyone in the school. And somehow, he simply seemed to stay up and float in the air without coming down. It's easy, he told me. You just jump as high as you can . . . and don't come down.

Basketball was his greatest joy in life. Even early on, he showed a talent. Those high jumps and gliding in air. But as a kid, he wasn't allowed to even watch high school basketball with whites.

One day, a friend's father bought him a ticket so he could watch the Harlem Globetrotters. It was a strike of lightning. He was totally captured. He decided on the spot that he was someday going to be a Harlem Globetrotter. It was burning in his bones.

He began to take the game seriously. His all-black high school team won the State Championship. He was captain of his team and named State All-American.

He decided to enroll at the University of Illinois. Financial assistance from the University made it possible for him to attend. He had no money. He was the first African American to play on the University's basketball team. The team was a national contender every year while Mannie was playing.

He remembers the cheers and the applause. But he remembers something else more poignantly. He and I are talking over a cup of coffee. As he tells the story, his eyes well up. Even telling the story causes him great pain.

"I was never allowed to eat with the team. Usually, they put me in another room to eat by myself. Then one day in this one restaurant, they made me eat in the kitchen. There was a window where I could see the rest of the team, eating, joking, poking themselves in fun. And here I was, alone. And no one, not one of my teammates, came to join me for dinner. It broke my heart."

But it didn't hold Mannie back. It might have crushed a lesser person. "I think those pains instilled hope in me. And faith in who I am. And a commitment to reach the top." Mannie's enthusiasm for life never lagged. Nor his determination to succeed. His was the human soul on fire.

It was often not an easy journey. Life is like that, always supplying thorns with the roses. There were disappointments, and times when the color of his skin blocked a promotion. He maintained his enthusiasm, however, during both the highs and the lows. That was a unique strength.

He understood the words of Frank Sinatra's refrain, "Each time I find myself lying flat on my face, I just pick myself up and get back in the race." For him, life was an adventure and he developed an endless enthusiasm and zest for every part of it.

His fondest dream came true. He played for the Harlem Globetrotters from 1962 to 1964. At the end of that season he decided that being a Globetrotter wasn't a lifetime job. He had to go to work.

Mannie climbs the corporate ladder and ends up at Honeywell. He becomes executive vice president of the corporation. But all the time he is working and becoming more and more successful, he keeps thinking about the Harlem Globetrotters. He dreams about them.

One day he decides he is going to buy the Globetrotters! There's no stopping him. He offers $6 million and they accept.

Mannie knows a thing or two about leadership. He brings that organization from near bankruptcy to the point where they are making a great deal of money.

And now, it's payback time. He has the money. And unbounded enthusiasm for his new mission. Mannie is not willing to creep when he feels the impulse to soar.

He builds and funds a youth center in Illmo, Missouri, where he grew up in the boxcar. He gives to a number of other organizations. But his great love is the University of Illinois. He decides that it will be one of the major areas of his philanthropy.

He establishes the Mannie L. Jackson Illinois Academic Enrichment and Leadership Program. That's a long name, but short on burdensome structure and process. It's an un-complicated one-on-one program.

Most of all, Mannie enjoys returning to the campus to handle the leadership sessions. At the University, Mannie instills in these young people a zest for life. He does the same all over the country for groups of over a thousand—at major conferences, corporations, and the like.

Mannie's enthusiasm is his defining characteristic. When he speaks to students in the program he established, his energy and excitement about life can be felt across the room. In some ways, it is truly amazing when you think of where he came from. And it is this quality that gives us the Twenty-Fourth Law of Relationships: *Enthusiasm is contagious.*

Enthusiasm is a great word. *En* comes from the Greek word for "within." *Thusiasm* comes from the Greek word *theos*, the word for "god." The original meaning of *enthusiastic*, therefore, was to have God within you.

That's Mannie Jackson—bursting with energy. What's most remarkable is that his enthusiasm is evident all the time, even when the chips are down. It's easy to be enthusiastic about life when everything is going well. But when you face troubles or suffering, it's hard to keep it up.

Come with me to one of those meetings where Mannie meets with all of his scholarship students. There they are, all sitting on the floor waiting for Mannie to enter the room. He walks to the center, surrounded by these young people. There's that glow of enthusiasm from him. They feed it back. They are so excited.

Now they are on their feet. Clapping. Cheering. *Mannie. Mannie!* The chant goes on.

His speech is exhilarating. Challenging. Inspiring. Motivating.

But that's not what you notice most of all. It's the enthusiasm displayed by Mannie for what he is achieving in these young people. And it's their enthusiasm for Mannie.

Your own enthusiasm influences everyone around you. It attracts others to you. It makes people want to be in a relationship with you.

The more you give of your enthusiasm, the more it spreads and the more that is returned to you. Enthusiasm is contagious. Start an epidemic.

Great enthusiasm makes you a force of nature. It inspires commitment. It moves those around you to action. Always follow the Twenty-Fourth Law of Relationships: *Enthusiasm is contagious.*

### How to Put the Twenty-Fourth Law into Practice

*"Enthusiasm is contagious."*

Enthusiasm cannot be overrated. When it comes to attracting others to you and building powerful relationships, it's your secret weapon.

Here are six ways to show and use your enthusiasm:

1. *When meeting with clients and customers.* If you're not enthusiastic about your job, about your organization, and about the product or service you represent, why would a prospect be excited?
2. *When interviewing for a job or applying for anything.* Are you knowledgeable about your prospective employer and enthusiastic about their business? Does it show?
3. *To inspire your employees.* If you're not excited about your organization's mission and strategy, why would your employees be?
4. *To encourage others when they're down.* Enthusiasm for the person and their strong qualities can help when things are dark.
5. *When you wake up in the morning.* What motivates you to get out of bed in the morning? Find something that you can be enthusiastic about and it will have a positive halo around everything else you do during the day.
6. *In building your social network.* What kind of person do you like to spend time with? A dismal complainer who criticizes others? Or someone who is enthusiastic and charged up about life? Enthusiasm gives you an attractive aura.

# 25

# Build It First

It's 7 a.m. and I'm checking my email. According to the experts, this is not the best way to start your day. But I can't resist the urge. I sip my coffee and slowly wake up. I scan the subject lines of a column of messages. The top two catch my eye. They are perfect examples of the value of investing in your relationships with people before you need help from them.

Here's how the first one starts: "I hope you will agree to help me launch my new book. I am sending you a copy. I'd like to ask you to write a five-star review on Amazon.com."

Now, I enjoy lending a hand to other authors. I do it often. But I've never met nor heard of this person. This gentleman wants me to commit significant time to helping him, but he hasn't laid the groundwork for his request.

I do a quick check.

No, he has never reviewed any of my books, or commented on my blog or website (that would have been a nice way to get my attention). He has never subscribed to any of my newsletters, or emailed me about how much he enjoyed one (flattery will get you everywhere!). Turns out, he is not even a friend of a friend (that kind of connection is always helpful, and you can often find one through LinkedIn or other social media platforms).

With very little effort the author of this email could have predisposed me to write that review for him.

Now the second email. It's from a fellow I went to graduate school with. I remember him as a nice person, although we were never particularly friendly at school. I have not heard from him in 30 years. He is starting a business and wants to know if I would like to invest in his new startup. The email is nearly 10 pages long and basically contains his entire business plan. Not a quick overview of the venture—the whole shooting match! He wants my cash.

This former classmate has a connection with me, and I respect that. But he has not contacted me in 30 years. He knows nothing about my goals in life, the state of my business, or my finances (important things to know if you're asking for money). He hasn't tried to find out if I have any natural interest in the service he hopes to offer (a good thing to find out when you're looking for investors).

He has not even bothered to ask me, in a brief, prior email, if I would be interested in receiving more information about his proposed new business idea. (Remember that time-tested strategy of evoking someone's *curiosity* to know more about the thing you're selling?)

It's not always necessary to do all this preparatory work before asking someone for something. An unexpected request, with no prior relationship, will sometimes be looked on favorably. But usually it helps to fertilize the soil beforehand.

I heard a very different story on a recent Southwest Airlines flight to Los Angeles. After you read this, you may be more willing to talk to your seatmate on your next flight. You never know who is traveling next to you.

I'm sitting in the aisle seat. The middle seat next to me is open. You know the feeling! I am hoping no one will sit there. And if someone does, I desperately hope they are petite, because three big men do not fit very comfortably in a row of economy seats. But the plane is filling up. One by one the incoming passengers walk by our row. No takers so far.

But then, a very tall, large man stops in the aisle at our row. "You aren't going to be very happy, but that's my seat," he announces, knowing how window and aisle seat passengers covet an empty middle seat. I'm dismayed. But he says it with a twinkle in his eyes and a lighthearted tone, which disarms me.

After the plane takes off, we start chatting. My companion must be six feet six inches tall. He is in his early 50s and African-American. He extends his hand to me. "I'm Petri," he says. "Petri Byrd." I do not recognize him. He tells me he's an actor in Los Angeles.

I ask him a question—a power question—that I often use with people who are well into their careers. "So, Petri, how did you get your start in acting?" I figure he'll talk about working summer stock in western Massachusetts, or acting in college plays. This is what Petri Byrd tells me:

"I was raised in Brooklyn, New York. I started my career as a bailiff in the Brooklyn circuit court of New York. Well, in the mid-80s I moved over to the Family Court Division. My judge was named Judy Sheindlin. I developed a very good, strong relationship with her during that time. I did my share in helping her run a tight ship in her courtroom."

"Huh," was all I could muster. I had not yet made the connection. "Then what happened? What about the acting? Were you taking acting classes at night or something?"

"I got my criminal justice degree from John Jay College. Then, around 1990, my wife and I decided to move to the West Coast. We wanted a fresh start for ourselves. I knew that my former judge from New York had moved out to Los Angeles herself and was looking into starting up a TV show. I called her and left a voice message. I said, 'Judy, I still look pretty good in uniform. If you ever need a bailiff, let me know.' I figured nothing would come of it, but it was worth a try."

Then it hit me. "You mean, this is Judge Judy? As in the TV show?"

"Yeah, exactly," Petri says with nonchalance. No smirk or rebuke for my ignorance. Petri is just an easygoing, regular guy. No big ego. No need for special treatment.

"I get a call the next day from Judy. She tells me she's looking for a bailiff. I meet with her, and I get the job on the spot. I had never acted before. It didn't matter. That had been my job. I knew how to do it for real—I didn't need acting lessons! So, that's how I got started. I've been her bailiff for over 10 years. I'm the longest running bailiff in court TV history. It's opened up lots of other opportunities for me."

Judge Judy's show is not just the highest rated courtroom TV show—it is the most popular show on daytime television in the United States. Number one! And Petri Byrd is her one and only bailiff. Every day, millions of people watch Judge Judy and her bailiff, Petri Byrd, on TV.

Imagine a different version of this story. What if the message on Judge Judy's phone had sounded like this (okay, suspend your disbelief for a minute): "Hi, I'm Petri Byrd and I'd like a job as your bailiff on your new TV show. I know you only have one bailiff spot open, and over 3,000 people have applied, but I'm the one. You've never heard of me. You've never met me. I've never done a thing for you. I've never followed your work. But I want your help."

He might have had a shot. But I don't think Petri would be telling me this if that had been the scenario.

Petri Byrd's story, told to me on a flight from Albuquerque to Los Angeles, highlights the Twenty-Fifth Law of Relationships: *Build your network before you need it.*

Invest in other people before you ask them for anything. Cultivate your relationships over time, the same way you would tend a garden. Don't be a freeloader who sees their network as a piggy bank.

(By the way—there is one exception to this Relationship Law. That's when the distance between you and the person you want to connect with is vast. If you haven't been able to cultivate a prior relationship with the person, the Second Law takes precedence—*Be unafraid to ask.* Read about it in Chapter 2.)

Two thousand years ago, the very first thing that the Romans did in each country they conquered was to build networks of beautifully engineered roads. They were constructed so well that some endure to this day. They created these roads well in advance of their future requirements for military and commercial transportation. In the same way, you must build your own network of relationships—your roads— in advance of your future career and personal needs.

Follow the Twenty-Fifth Law of Relationships—*Build your network before you need it*—and all sorts of unexpected opportunities will come your way. You will find that a helping hand is rarely more than a phone call away.

## How to Put the Twenty-Fifth Law into Practice

*"Build your network before you need it."*

Here are four simple but powerful steps you can take to develop your network:

1. You cannot possibly manage your entire network of contacts in the same way. Divide your professional network into three groups:
   - The Critical Few (15–20 people)
   - The Middle Few (25–75 people)
   - The Many (everyone else—hundreds or thousands)
2. Create a staying-in-touch plan that's feasible and appropriate for each group. For example:
   - Talk to your *Critical Few* group two to three times a year. Stay in close touch, and invest to understand their needs.
   - Contact the *Middle Few* periodically. At least once a year, use personalized communications (cards, letters, personal emails, phone calls, etc.).
   - Use low-labor intensive ways to stay connected with *The Many*—the hundreds or thousands of contacts you have. These could include things like an article mailing, a newsletter, a blog, and so on.
3. Once or twice a year, manually scroll through your entire contact database. Be on the lookout for names of people you ought to get in contact with. Flag them.
4. Always search for ways to help and encourage the people in your network.

# 26

# A Pebble in a
# Pond

I call it the *ripple effect*.

Think of throwing a pebble into a pond. Watch the ripples fanning out. Each circle a little larger than the one before. Ever growing. Keep the ripple effect in mind as I tell you the story of Richard Goldbach. It involves the most frightening moment in his life.

I'm having breakfast with Rich. I am an overnight guest in his home. It is one of the most beautifully furnished homes I've ever seen. It is like visiting a museum.

Rich was CEO and majority owner of Metro Machine. Under his leadership, the company grew into a large and very prosperous enterprise. General Dynamics had its eye on it for some time. It was finally purchased by them in 2011.

Rich is a very generous guy, a philanthropist of sorts. His company was located in Norfolk, Virginia. It was one of the largest contributors to the local United Way. And one of the largest contributors to the Boys & Girls Club of Norfolk.

He was also particularly interested in what he considered the most serious scourge in Norfolk's inner city. It became the largest beneficiary of his philanthropy. That is what this story is about.

Rich and his company were the sole contributors to a remarkable literacy program he initiated for grade school youngsters. The program was held in the worst-performing schools in the most disadvantaged neighborhoods of the inner city.

"I'm convinced," Rich tells me, "that if these young people learn to read and love to read, it gives them a head start in life. I think it is one of our major hopes for the future. For them. And for the country."

For Rich, there was love and commitment for this literacy program. Plus a great deal of money each year that went into the project. Over a million dollars a year.

Back now to that terrifying moment in Rich's life.

His company is in the business of shipbuilding and repairing nuclear propelled ships for the U.S. Navy. The plant is located on the waterfront. It is in a very difficult, robbery-afflicted, mostly abandoned part of Norfolk.

Rich is leaving work late one evening. It's a dark, chilly night. He walks toward his car in the unlit parking lot of his company.

In the darkness he glimpses something moving a few hundred feet ahead of him. It is a man. A very large man. Rich is thinking of avoiding him and getting to his car as fast as he can. He quickens the pace. The man is now angling directly toward Rich from across the parking lot. Rich reaches for his cell phone.

But the faster he walks, the faster the man comes toward him. He's gaining on Rich. This guy is big. As dark as it is outside, they are now so close that Rich sees the outline of the man quite clearly. And he doesn't like what he sees. And fears.

He thinks the worst. He has a valuable watch but not too much money. He knows he's probably going to have to give it all up. He quickly decides that's what he'll do. He just wants to come out of it alive.

Soon the man catches up with Rich. They're face to face. He hears the man's heavy breathing. Rich is frozen with fright. Paralyzed.

"Mr. Goldbach. Mr. Goldbach," the man calls out.

*How can he possibly know my name?* Rich wonders. He has probably singled me out. "I think he's been stalking me," Rich tells me.

"He grabs my arm. And then he reaches for my hand. He shakes my hand. Good grief, he is shaking my hand. He's talking to me.

" 'Mr. Goldbach, I just want to thank you. I owe you so much. You have taught my third-grade son to read. Now, Mr. Goldbach . . . he's teaching me to read.' "

As Rich tells me the story, he is choked with emotion. Even after all this time. In the canons of relationships, he is a sure candidate for sainthood.

There is no way of knowing how your relationship with a program or with an individual might create a ripple effect that influences many others. The circle expands. Dozens. Hundreds. Perhaps more. Andrew Gold wrote a song, "Thank You for Being a Friend."

When you help others, you end up touching many other lives. It's because of the Twenty-Sixth Law of Relationships: *Every act of generosity creates a ripple.*

Rich Goldbach experienced first hand how the ripple effect multiplied his generosity. Often, however, we don't see it. But don't be discouraged—the ripples caused by your actions may just be too far away for you to catch sight of them.

Your influence is greater than you think, but it doesn't always manifest itself in the ways you expect. The Twenty-Sixth Law of Relationships—*Every act of generosity creates a ripple*—ensures that your actions will have an impact well beyond what you can see.

## How to Put the Twenty-Sixth Law into Practice

### *"Every act of generosity creates a ripple."*

Generosity has the power to move people in extraordinary ways. Dr. Albert Schweitzer, the missionary who devoted his life to helping the sick in Africa, once said, "Do something wonderful. People may imitate it." He also wrote, "Example is leadership." You encourage generosity through your own example.

Here are five simple ways you can create more ripples through your relationships:

1. Call someone up—or stop and chat—with no other purpose than to ask them how they are. Tell them you're thinking about them and wondering how they are doing.
2. Let others get in front of you in a line, or in traffic. Wave them on!
3. Smile at the next waiter in a restaurant or clerk in a store. Ask them how they are. They're probably working long hours at low pay.
4. As you're able, give to causes you support and to people in need. Interestingly, research shows that Americans at lower and middle income levels give a greater percentage of their income to charity than those making over $100,000 a year. (Why do you think that is?)
5. Ask yourself what your purpose in life is. Why are you here? Your answer just may encourage you to focus more on the ripple effect you can have through your relationships.

# Applying the Laws

## OVERCOMING 16 COMMON
## RELATIONSHIP CHALLENGES

You've read about the 26 Laws of Relationships. Through the stories in each chapter, you've seen how they work. Now, you need to apply them to every aspect of your life.

The first thing you should do is download the free *Power Relationships* workbook we have created to help you create a personal relationship-building action plan. Go to andrewsobel.com or panaslinzy.com to get it immediately.

Then, read through this section. We've listed 16 common relationship challenges that people face. Most of these are professional challenges—for example, building more relationships with senior executives—but some pertain to friends and family. For each challenge, we list several of the Laws that are especially applicable. Then, we describe a series of steps that will help you meet that particular challenge.

Let's first review the 26 Relationship Laws:

1. Power relationships are based on great conversations, not one person showing the other how much they know.
2. Be unafraid to ask.
3. Follow the person, not the position.
4. The greatest gift is to believe in someone.
5. Know the other person's agenda and help them accomplish it.
6. Stretch yourself by building relationships with people quite different than you.
7. Serious engagement needs a relationship.
8. Integrity isn't important—it's everything.
9. Walk in the other person's shoes.

164

10. Don't be put off by an awkward start—find something personal that connects you and you may develop a wonderful relationship.
11. Give trust to get trust.
12. Change the environment and you'll deepen the relationship.
13. Don't wait to let someone know how much they mean to you.
14. There's always something, no matter how small, that you can do to help the people around you.
15. Treat a prospect like a client, and there's a good chance they'll become one.
16. Vulnerability is power.
17. To reach their fullest potential, people need both truth and love.
18. Make them curious.
19. Show you care, often, by giving recognition and praise.
20. It's better to know the right questions than to have all the answers.
21. A selfless motive creates powerful bonds.
22. Become part of your clients' growth and profits and they'll never get enough of you.
23. To succeed, you need a small group of people who trust you, believe in you, and are committed to you—not hundreds of superficial contacts.
24. Enthusiasm is contagious.
25. Build your network before you need it.
26. Every act of generosity creates a ripple.

## 16 COMMON RELATIONSHIP CHALLENGES

Here are the relationship challenges we're going to help you overcome:

### Client Relationships

1. How can I build more relationships in the C-suite and with top executives who are key decision makers?
2. I've been pigeonholed by my client—how do I expand their perception of my capabilities?
3. How do I build a relationship with a client who doesn't seem to want one?
4. How do I develop more personal relationships with my clients?

### Sales

5. How can I get more meetings with potential clients and customers?
6. How do I move from a casual conversation with a business contact to a discussion about how my products and services could help them?
7. What can I do when my sales process is stuck? I'm having lots of conversations but they don't seem to go anywhere.

### At Work

8. How do I build a strong relationship with my boss?
9. How do I get my colleagues to support me and help me succeed in my work?
10. How do I make time for building long-term relationships?
11. I'm looking for a job. How do I work my network and develop the sorts of connections that will help me?
12. How do I use social media to help grow my network?
13. I'm just setting out to build/rebuild my professional network. Where do I start?

## At Home

14. What will help rekindle the romance in my relationship with my spouse/partner?
15. How can I improve my relationships with my children and foster more communication?
16. I've been focused mainly on work and family and haven't developed my circle of friends—how can I strengthen my personal connections and friendships?

## CLIENT RELATIONSHIPS

## 1. How can I build more relationships in the C-suite and with top executives who are key decision makers?

**Laws That Will Help**

Law 3: *Follow the person, not the position.*

Many executives already have a well-established group of advisors and providers they work with, and it's hard to break in. Start now by building and maintaining relationships with up-and-comers—smart, ambitious individuals who will someday be in senior positions.

Law 18: *Make them curious.*

Top executives are assailed daily by people who want to meet with them. Make them curious to see you. Then, incite their interest about a topic that will draw them to want a follow-up meeting. That's important because getting the second meeting is often harder than getting the first meeting.

Law 22: *Become part of your clients' growth and profits and they'll never get enough of you.*

When you're considered an expense to be managed, clients will cut you at any time. But if your work is seen as helping to grow revenue, improve profits, and increase innovation, then clients will see a huge return on investment. C-suite executives in particular are focused on revenue and growth.

**Additional Actions**

1. Produce thought leadership that will appeal to C-suite executives. An article about your latest quality control methodology isn't really going to appeal to a chief financial officer. But an article entitled "Five Questions Every CEO Should Ask Before Outsourcing" just might get their attention.

2. Add value for time. Middle managers are concerned with value
   for money, but C-suite executives are focused on value for
   time when it comes to relationship building. What external
   insights can you bring about markets and competition? What
   ideas can you share about improving existing operations? Can
   you help the executive reframe the problem?
3. Try to establish a relationship with leadership at the very
   beginning of the sales process and then also during your
   ongoing work. Articulate to your day-to-day client why that
   exposure will help ensure the success of your engagement.
   Make sure you are able to frame your work in the context of
   the organization's overall goals and aspirations.

## 2. I've been pigeonholed by my client—how do I expand their perception of my capabilities?

### Laws That Will Help

Law 1: *Power relationships are based on great conversations, not one person trying to show the other how much they know.*
To broaden your client's perception of your capabilities, you must broaden your conversations. Stop spending all of your time talking about the current project and start having more expansive conversations with your client about their aspirations, goals, and the most challenging issues.

Law 12: *Change the environment and you'll deepen the relationship.*
When you create interactions with your client outside the office, it changes the relationship dynamics. People let their guard down and are more open. You talk about different things.

Law 20: *It's better to know the right questions than to have all the answers.*
Thoughtful questions are your most valuable tool for exploring a client's business and career challenges and getting to know them better. When you ask pertinent questions about possible problems or opportunities where you can offer solutions, it expands your client's perception of what you can do for them.

## Additional Actions

1. If you work with a firm or large company, make it a point of regularly introducing colleagues who have specialist expertise in an area of interest to the client.

2. Introduce your client to other clients who have used your full suite of services or products. Suggest a site visit so they can actually go and see how another client has used your solutions to deal with the same challenge.

3. Offer a capabilities showcase. Use multimedia and create a highly interactive session where a client can see and experience the full range of your work.

4. Lower your threshold for a client meeting. By spending more informal time with clients, you'll learn more about their needs and frustrations.

5. Take a deep dive into an issue of interest to your client. Set up a formal discussion to walk through an in-depth perspective or set of research findings that you bring to the table.

## 3. How do I build a relationship with a client who doesn't seem to want one?

### Laws That Will Help

Law 6: *Stretch yourself by building relationships with people quite different than you.*

Think of the difficult client as a challenge. It may seem like the other person doesn't want a relationship. They probably have a different character and temperament compared with you. But have you really tried to connect with them, consistently, over time? Have you stretched yourself?

Law 9: *Walk in the other person's shoes.*

Even people who are standoffish will build a relationship with someone who is meeting their needs and helping them accomplish their goals. Do you really understand this client's hot buttons and concerns?

Law 15: *Treat a prospect like a client, and there's a good chance they'll become one.*

For this challenge, this law has a slightly broader meaning. Most people distance themselves from someone when the relationship is difficult or awkward. In this case, try to act as though this is one of your best clients. Your positive, helpful attitude will invariably improve the situation.

### Additional Actions

1. Refocus on the client's agenda. Make sure you really understand what they are trying to achieve.
2. Clarify or recalibrate expectations for the work at hand. What outcomes do they seek? What kind of communications does this client expect? How often do they want to meet?
3. Find out if this person has a trusted relationship with another outside provider or with a particular colleague. What characterizes that relationship?
4. Consider that this may be one of those individuals who simply won't develop more than an arm's-length relationship with an advisor or supplier outside their company. In that case, do a good job for the client but invest your time in building other, more promising relationships.

## 4. How do I develop more personal relationships with my clients?

### Laws That Will Help

Law 16: *Vulnerability is power.*

Emotional vulnerability creates more intimacy in a relationship. You have to be willing—in appropriate and non-intrusive ways—

to access other people's feelings and to disclose your own. The goal is emotional resonance.

Law 20: *It's better to know the right questions than to have all the answers.*

To build a personal relationship, you need to learn about the other person and they need to learn more about you. Your best tool to do this is thoughtful questions.

Law 21: *A selfless motive creates powerful bonds.*

You must be sincerely interested in the other person. You can't be trying to get close to someone for purely mercenary motivations.

## Additional Actions

1. Follow your client's lead. Move slowly and take small steps. If someone is very private, gradually build familiarity.

2. Be intensely curious. Take a keen interest in other people and their lives. Ask questions—about their interests, their families, their aspirations, their vacations, their opinions, their views on current events, and so on. "How did you get your start?" can be a good opener.

3. Look for similarities and commonalities and use them to connect. Connect with clients around common interests, family, mutual acquaintances, and life's concerns and challenges.

4. Invest in face time to build familiarity. Particularly at the beginning of a relationship, it's important to build up a reservoir of face-to-face interactions. Familiarity leads to likeability and trust.

5. Be human and accessible. Show confidence tempered by humility. Admit that you may have been wrong in your opinion about something or someone.

## SALES

### 5. How can I get more meetings with potential clients and customers?

#### Laws That Will Help

Law 2: *Be unafraid to ask.*

Many senior executives will not meet with someone they don't know already or who has not been recommended to them. However, if you are creative, bold, and persistent, you may be able to get through.

Law 18: *Make them curious.*

The best way to get a prospective client to meet with you is to evoke their curiosity about your ability to solve a problem they have. When a prospect is curious, they will "reach" toward you instead of feeling sold to. Are you clearly showing how you can solve a problem that your potential clients have?

Law 25: *Build your network before you need it.*

If a prospect already knows you and has found you helpful, they will be more willing to meet. You'll get a much warmer reception when you want to discuss business.

#### Additional Actions

1. Create value-added content that demonstrates your expertise in helping clients address specific problems and challenges. Regularly get it in front of your network in multiple formats—blogs, articles, white papers, checklists, diagnostic tools, and videos.

2. Comb through your various networks and identify possible prospects or pathfinders. Go through your email for the last couple of years, look at your social media connections, review your alumni networks, and cull out possible contacts.

3. Ask current and past clients, and others who know you well, for referrals to get warm introductions to prospects. Cold calling should be your last resort.

4. Approach each prospect in a way that will pique their curiosity. Show how what you offer will help them achieve their goals. Offer to share interesting research, market data, or unique information about an important issue they face.

5. Make at least one "outreach" per day to your network, preferably two or three. In a few months you can grow your stream of warm leads significantly.

## 6. How do I move from a casual conversation with a business contact to a discussion about how my products and services could help them?

### Laws That Will Help

Law 1: *Power relationships are based on great conversations, not one person showing the other how much they know.*

When talking to a business contact, have an interesting conversation—don't try to impress them or get personal too quickly. Ask the other person questions about their work and their challenges, and share—briefly—what you do.

Law 5: *Know the other person's agenda and help them accomplish it.*
At the heart of developing relationships is an understanding of the other person's agenda of priorities, needs, and goals (both professional and personal). When you understand their agenda, you will then know how you can add value.

Law 15: *Treat a prospect like a client, and there's a good chance they'll become one.*

Your conversations with contacts in your network shouldn't look all that different than your conversations with your clients. Basically, you're trying to help them. You build personal rapport and trust. You ask thoughtful questions that clarify the other person's issues. You bring to life how you help clients by describing examples of your work. You share best practices. You add value.

### Additional Actions

1. Steer the conversation so that you understand what the other person's most important goals and challenges are. When you're finished talking, say, "Those are the kinds of issues I help my clients solve, and I'd be happy to buy you lunch and have a follow-up discussion."

2. Based on what you learn, immediately ask yourself, "How can I help this person?" Are they brand new in their job? Send them an article or book on getting started in a new position. Are they new to town and looking at schools for their children? Steer them to the right expert. And so on.

3. Share what you do with others in an interesting, engaging manner. Don't lecture, use jargon, or ramble on for five minutes. When you are asked what you do, state your value proposition ("I'm an accountant. I help my clients get their taxes done on time, without errors, and with a reduced risk of an audit.").

## 7. What can I do when my sales process is stuck? I'm having lots of conversations but they don't seem to go anywhere.

### Laws That Will Help

Law 7: *Serious engagement needs a relationship.*
Have you really established a proper relationship of trust that can facilitate the sale?

Law 9: *Walk in the other person's shoes.*
You see a problem that can be fixed and you don't understand why the client doesn't just move ahead to address it. But have

you really walked in their shoes? Have you reflected on the organizational constraints they may be up against, or the difficulties they face in aligning stakeholders? Do a better job of understanding these.

Law 10: *Don't be put off by an awkward start—find something personal that connects you, and you may develop a wonderful relationship.*

A sale is rarely made on the first call. Sometimes a relationship has to develop over many months or even years before you'll get the sale. In addition to promoting the value and impact of what you are offering, look for personal commonalities.

## Additional Actions

Review the five preconditions for a prospect (or existing client) to become a buyer:

1. They perceive a significant problem or opportunity. (If there isn't one, why would they hire you or buy from you?)
2. The executive you're talking to "owns" the issue and can take action. (You're wasting your time if the prospect can't personally move ahead.)
3. There is a healthy dissatisfaction with the rate of improvement and/or with existing providers. (They may have a problem but feel it's being adequately addressed by current efforts.)
4. They trust that you are the best, highest-value alternative. (Preconditions 1–3 could all be present, but in the end the prospect has to have full trust in your ability to address their issue.)
5. They feel the right stakeholders are aligned to go ahead. (In most large organizations, a buyer must ensure that key influencers are in agreement with the decision to hire you.)

## AT WORK

## 8. How do I build a strong relationship with my boss?

### Laws That Will Help

Law 5: *Know the other person's agenda and help them accomplish it.*
You need to understand your boss's agenda of critical priorities and goals. A positive relationship will be based, first of all, on how well you help them to accomplish these through the specific expectations that have been set for you.

Law 20: *It's better to know the right questions than to have all the answers.*
By asking thoughtful and thought-provoking questions that help uncover improvement opportunities, you'll earn a reputation as a strong, proactive thinker.

Law 24: *Enthusiasm is contagious.*
Employers prize enthusiasm and energy. Your job is to help your boss and your organization succeed, and you should look for every opportunity to do so. Don't be depressed and whiny on the job!

### Additional Actions

1. Find out how your boss will be evaluated at the end of the year by his boss. What metrics are being used to measure his performance? Make sure you demonstrate how your work is supporting one or more of these.
2. Don't create a narrow definition of your role and then stick stubbornly to it. Be willing to help anywhere, anytime, with any task—no matter how seemingly trivial. That attitude will put you in good stead with anyone you work with.
3. Anytime you have a planning or operational review meeting, spend time crafting two to three powerful questions to ask. You'll come across as a thoughtful, strategic thinker.

4. Understand your boss as a person. You won't become their friend, but you need to understand their values, upbringing, risk tolerance, personal network, and so on. Begin with, "How did you get your start?"

## 9. How do I get my colleagues to support me and help me succeed in my work?

### Laws That Will Help

Law 4: *The greatest gift is to believe in someone.*
Are you supportive of your colleagues? Do you criticize them or do you build them up and praise their abilities and potential? Would they say you believe in them?

Law 5: *Know the other person's agenda and help them accomplish it.*
If you want your colleagues to help you, you have to help them. To do that, you have to understand their priorities and needs. Have you invested the time to discover what they are?

Law 21: *A selfless motive creates powerful bonds.*
The worst reputation you can possibly have is as someone who just looks out for his or herself. Do you share credit where it's due—or, even, err on the side of giving others more credit than you even think they deserve? (Not infrequently, we overestimate our own contributions.)

### Additional Actions

1. Get to know your colleagues as people. You don't have to become their best friend, but you should understand who they are and what's important to them.
2. Each week, spend 15 minutes with someone you don't know well at work. Ask them what they're working on. Find out what their agenda is. In a year you'll make nearly fifty new or deeper connections.

3. Go out of your way to find opportunities to help a colleague who is facing a tough challenge or otherwise could use a helping hand. Is someone facing an impending deadline or trying to finish a difficult project? Offer to support them.

## 10. How do I make time for building long-term relationships?

### Laws That Will Help

Law 3: *Follow the person, not the position.*

There are two important implications of this law for this particular challenge: First, you need to be tracking a defined, identified network of contacts. This enables you to approach the task systematically. Second, you must take a long-term perspective. You may need business right now—and you need to act on that—but you must always be developing your relationships for the long term.

Law 25: *Build your network before you need it.*

It's actually easier to make time for building relationships when you are not under pressure to connect with someone or make a sale. If you do it week in, week out, you'll find the time commitment is manageable—and over time you'll make huge progress.

### Additional Actions

1. Make a commitment. Resolve to elevate the quality of your *relationships* to the same level as your *professional* or vocational mastery.

2. Think about an ongoing process, not an event. Treat relationship building as you would diet and exercise. Neither is a one-off event that takes place on January 1 to kick off the New Year. Both succeed through a lifestyle change—that is, the daily discipline to do small things on a regular basis.

3. Focus. Put significant focus on your "critical few" relation-ships—those 15 to 25 relationships that will really make a difference—not on every name in your contact database. Keep this list on your desk or in your pocket at all times.
4. Schedule weekly activities. Treat *yourself* like a client and schedule time each week in your agenda for "important but not urgent" long-term relationship-building and personal brand-building efforts.
5. Create small rituals. For example: Come in early one day a week to work on your short list of key relationships; send one card a day to someone in your network; write a short summary of every client meeting and send it to the partic-ipants the next day; spend 10 minutes each week with a colleague you don't know well; and so on.
6. Enlist others to help you. Use an administrative assistant or junior team member to extend your reach and help keep track of key individuals—use your assignment as a "relation-ship marketing manager." Get your team involved, so that everyone working on a client engagement has relationship-building responsibilities.
7. Work smarter not harder. Using existing interactions with clients more productively: Ask them about their issues, their backgrounds, and their aspirations.
8. Piggyback where possible. Increase the productivity of trips and visits to different cities by holding one additional meeting with a contact or potential client before you leave town.

## 11. I'm looking for a job. How do I work my network and develop the sorts of connections that will help me?

### Laws That Will Help
Law 2: *Be unafraid to ask.*
At the same time you are asking those closest to you for help and suggestions, you need to be audacious and unafraid to ask. Call

people at the periphery of your network—they may be able to connect you to entirely new networks. In a famous study on job hunting, a sociologist found that these "weak links" were very important in finding a new job.

Law 22: *Become part of your client's growth and profits and they'll never get enough of you.*

In this case, the Twenty-Second Law encourages you to focus on how you can help the people around you grow and prosper. How can you further their highest-level goals? If you're speaking to a potential employer, are you giving them ideas for how they can grow and improve their business?

Law 23: *To succeed, you need a small group of people who trust you, believe in you, and are committed to you—not hundreds of superficial contacts.*

Now is the time to draw on your inner circle. If you don't have a strong inner circle, you need to develop one. Who are your "loyalists"—your staunchest supporters?

## Additional Actions

1. Begin by interviewing for information. If you're calling to see if someone has a job opening, you're going to get turned down 99 percent of the time. But if you're calling to get advice and learn, you'll get a much warmer reception.

2. End every conversation by asking for one or two more names of people you should speak to.

3. Many employers are putting their focus on interviewing candidates who have been recommended by employees. Work this channel and speak to all your contacts who are working for organizations that might be appropriate for you. Being referred to a recruiter will vastly improve your odds of getting an interview.

4. If you're recently out of school and are still unemployed, think about getting the experiences that will make you attractive to employers a year or two from now. If you're working a minimum wage job in order to get by, supplement that

with other activities like studying for a professional certification, working at a nonprofit, and so on. You need to show you're doing everything possible to get into your chosen field.

## 12. How do I use social media to grow my network?

### Laws That Will Help

Law 2: *Be unafraid to ask.*

Social media gives you unprecedented opportunities to reach out and expand your network. You can ask people you don't know yet to connect with you on LinkedIn or Facebook, and there are many places on the Web that you can ask for information, advice, help, etc. as a first and legitimate interaction with someone you may want to meet.

Law 8: *Integrity isn't important—it's everything.*

It's easy to be dishonest on social media—and also to get uncovered as a fake. Fact-checking is easier than it's ever been. Your social media presence is now part of your brand and persona, and dishonesty will not just be found out but it will hurt you for a long time to come.

Law 24: *Enthusiasm is contagious.*

When people are enthusiastic about something on the Web, it goes viral quickly. In this example, the Twenty-Fourth Law can be activated by making others enthusiastic about your writing, your products and services, and your ideas in general.

### Additional Actions

1. Do a self-assessment of your use of social media. A few years ago social media platforms were more of a novelty, but today they are well established. For example, at the time of this writing, there are 1.1 billion monthly Facebook users; 288 million monthly active Twitter users; 359 million monthly Google+ users; and over 200 million users of LinkedIn (Source: GlobalWebIndex study). Which of these platforms

are you using today? Are they helping you form new connections and deepen existing ones? Which do you want to develop and actively participate in?

2. Use services such as LinkedIn and Google+ to identify natural network extension opportunities. These could be professional groups (e.g., IT professionals), alumni groups, company groups, or other affinity groups that you could join and participate in.

3. Think of social media as a way to get to know someone before you eventually meet in person. The knowledge you build about each other online will help accelerate your relationship once you meet face to face.

4. Don't overinvest in social media to the detriment of building deep relationships with your inner circle of "critical few" contacts. When you face important issues and challenges in your career and life, you will go to your deepest relationships for help, not a bunch of online friends or contacts you hardly know.

## 13. I'm just setting out to build/rebuild my professional network. Where do I start?

### Laws That Will Help

Law 3: *Follow the person, not the position.*

Take a very long-term perspective when developing your network. That entry-level manager you're working with today may very well be able to purchase your products or services in five years. And in 10 or 15 years, they could be the CEO.

Law 14: *There's always something, no matter how small, that you can do to help the people around you.*

Build a reputation as someone who is always willing to help a friend or colleague. Your network will grow rapidly.

Law 23: *To succeed, you need a handful of people who trust you, believe in you, and are committed to you—not hundreds of superficial contacts.* There are many benefits to building a broad network that may ultimately include hundreds or thousands of contacts. However, never forget that in the end, you are going to need a handful of close, trusted relationships in order to thrive.

## Additional Actions

1. Define a series of networks that you want to stay in touch with—for example, alumni from your college or graduate school, former employees of a company you used to work for, professional or functional groups, and so on.
2. Attend events—selectively—that are relevant to the network you are trying to build. Pick two or three a year. Don't overdo generalized "networking," however.
3. Develop relationships broadly within your own company. Remember, in 10 years many of the individuals you know there will be working elsewhere, and you'll want them to be part of your network.
4. Work your social media platforms, but don't think that Facebook "friends" or LinkedIn connections are substitutes for real relationships. Use social media to get to know people before you meet them in person—this can accelerate the relationship-building process.
5. Always find out what others' interests and goals are, and note these. For those you really want to stay in touch with, follow up from time to time with something valued-added that connects to their agenda (an article, an introduction to someone else in your network, etc.).
6. Be interested in everyone you meet. Remember Dale Carnegie's famous quote: "You will be more successful by being interested in others' success than by trying to get them interested in your success."

## AT HOME

### 14. What will help rekindle the romance in my relationship with my spouse/partner?

**Laws That Will Help**

Law 4: *The greatest gift is to believe in someone.*

Does your spouse, deep down, feel that you truly believe in them? Unequivocally and without reservations? When we start out in life, our parents—sometimes one or the other—are the people who have that rock-solid, steadfast belief in us. Later, it's often a spouse or partner who provides that deep well of confidence that no other human being can give us to the same degree.

Law 13: *Don't wait to let someone know how much they mean to you.*

Gary Chapman, author of the perennial bestseller *The 5 Love Languages*, points out that people express their love in different ways. Some of us affirm it verbally, some through physical touch, yet others through acts of service. You may have been expressing how much the other person means to you through these other, non-verbal means. But sometimes, you need to *say it*—especially if that's your partner's own means of expressing love.

Law 19: *Show you care, often, by giving recognition and praise.*

Do you praise your partner often? Or, do you tend to point out what they are doing wrong? Dr. John Gottman, probably the leading authority on marriage, has conducted the most extensive research on what makes for a successful union and on the factors that lead to divorce. He has found that two of the four absolute predictors of a breakup are showing *contempt* and being *critical* toward your spouse (the other two are stonewalling and defensiveness).

## Additional Actions

1. Start with questions. Organize a quiet dinner for just the two of you. Ask things like:

   ■ *What are your dreams?* Allow some silence. Ask this question with no elaboration—don't ruin it with other words. Then wait.

   ■ *What would you say has been the happiest day of your life?* (And, why did you choose that day?) Think of this question as the start of a much longer conversation. Why did they choose that particular day? What other days have been happy ones? What is happiness, for him or her, anyway? Is it the same thing as joy or contentment?

   ■ *Can you tell me about your plans?* We are all so full of our own plans. When we really, truly focus on our partner— and not just use what he or she says as a springboard to talk about ourselves—we learn amazing things.

   ■ *What do you wish you could spend more time on each week? Less time?* This question can reveal a lot about your partner's likes and dislikes. It can highlight what's important to them, and suggest opportunities to shift their priorities.

   ■ *Right now, what are you most passionate or excited about in your life?* When you tap into people's passions, they come alive and the conversation comes alive. All of a sudden you're not just chitchatting about superficial trivia. You're talking about the stuff that lights us on fire.

   ■ *What are you doing this week that I could help you with or support you on?* Even if the answer is nothing, you'll make the other person feel supported and loved. If there is something—well, it's a good day when you can identify how to help someone else.

2. Schedule small rituals. It could be a conversation every Sunday night about your upcoming week's schedule, reading time together after dinner, or a regular evening out each week.

3. Use the Twelfth Law and change the relationship environment. Go somewhere new together. Get out of the house.

## 15. How can I improve my relationships with my children and foster more communication?

### Laws That Will Help

Law 9: *Walk in the other person's shoes.*
Law 9 helps you empathize. *You* may feel that the experiences your child is going through are routine or minor ("everyone experiences that!"), but to your child they may feel overwhelming. If the person you're talking to doesn't feel you understand what they're going through, they'll shut you out and won't listen.

Law 16: *Vulnerability is power.*
To teenagers or young adults, it can look like their grown-up parents have it all together. You can increase rapport and intimacy by shedding some of that veneer and showing you're human and fallible. Psychologists say it can be helpful to share your own feelings about how to act toward them. For example: "I feel a bit of a dilemma. On the one hand, I want you to experience independence and be in charge of your life. On the other, and in this particular situation, I feel protective toward you and want to help you make the right choices. . . ."

Law 21: *A selfless motive creates powerful bonds.*
One definition of "enablement" is trying to control the other person under the guise that it's in their best interests. When dealing with your own children, you have to examine your motives. Are you genuinely focused on what's right for them? Spoiling a child could very well be done to serve yourself, for example, your own need to be loved, rather than their interests.

**Additional Actions**

1. Connect on their terms, not yours. As children get older, it can be harder to get them motivated to spend time with you. Ask what interests *them* and what they'd like to do and see— as opposed to imposing your own particular interests on them. You might like baseball or visiting a museum, but they may prefer going to a skateboarding park with you.

2. Don't force communication, especially with teenagers. Rather, create opportunities for relaxed face time. A long car trip, going to a sporting event, or a family vacation oriented around a common interest will allow you to talk in a relaxed setting and gain a better understanding of what's on their minds. Asking a teenager after a day at school, "How are you doing?" will usually get a superficial response ("Fine. Why do you keep asking?").

3. Withhold judgment. When people—and especially children—feel judged, they withdraw. If your teenager makes a mistake or shows bad judgment, don't ask, "Why did you do that?" (which is really saying, "Why were you so stupid?"). Instead, ask something such as, "What do you think you ought to do now?" or "What did you learn from that?"

## 16. I've been focused mainly on work and family and haven't developed my circle of friends—how can I strengthen my personal connections and friendships?

**Laws That Will Help**

Law 10: *Don't be put off by an awkward start—find something personal that connects you and you may develop a wonderful relationship.*

The second half of this law is the important part for this challenge. The easiest way to reconnect with friends is through your common interests. Recall that the story behind this law revolves around two people (the president of Yale and a wealthy philanthropist) who bonded through two shared interests: their fathers, who went to Yale together, and their love of baseball.

Law 26: *Every act of generosity creates a ripple.*

A small gesture can help rekindle a friendship, especially when you reach out to someone with no self-interest.

## Additional Actions

1. Find small things you can do to show an interest in your friends. Visit someone who's going through a rough patch. Send someone else a book that you enjoyed—it's easy to do with online booksellers. Just call a friend up and ask them how they are, with no agenda and no need to talk about yourself.

2. Start treating yourself like a client. Schedule time with friends and family that is as sacrosanct as an important client engagement. Do it well in advance. If your schedule for the next month is packed, invite some friends over in two months' time.

3. Prioritize. Whom do you really want to stay in touch with this year and maintain or deepen your relationship with? Do you feel an obligation to spend time with some people due to historic connections that no longer make sense? Do you continue to see some people simply out of a feeling of guilt or responsibility?

# About the Authors

This is the second book that Andrew Sobel and Jerry Panas have coauthored together. Their collaboration has worked well because they followed three of the Relationship Laws you've read about in *Power Relationships*:

Law 6: *Stretch yourself by building relationships with people quite different than you.* From differences comes strength. Think Felix and Oscar from *The Odd Couple*.

Law 7: *Serious engagement needs a relationship.* The authors knew each other for years before writing their first book together. This relationship provided the foundation for successful teamwork.

Law 23: *To succeed, you need a small group of people who trust you, believe in you, and are committed to you—not hundreds of superficial contacts.* Andrew and Jerry would each consider the other to be part of their inner circle of trusted relationships.

## Andrew Sobel

Andrew is the most widely published author in the world on client loyalty and the capabilities required to build trusted business relationships. His first book, the bestselling *Clients for Life*, defined an entire genre of business literature about client loyalty. His other books include *Power Questions*, which has been translated into eight languages and spent 52 weeks on the Bookscan National Business Bestseller list; *Making Rain*; and the award-winning *All for One*.

For 30 years, Andrew has worked as both a consultant to senior management and an executive educator and coach. His clients have included leading corporations such as Citigroup, Xerox, and Cognizant; as well as professional service firms such as Ernst & Young, Booz Allen Hamilton, Towers Watson, and many others. His articles and work have been featured in a variety of publications such as *The New York Times*, *Business Week*, and the *Harvard Business Review*. Andrew is a graduate of Middlebury College, and earned his MBA at Dartmouth's Tuck School.

Andrew is an acclaimed keynote speaker who delivers idea-rich, high-energy speeches and seminars at major conferences and events. His topics include "Developing Clients for Life," "Building Power Relationships," "Creating a Rainmaking Firm," "The Beatles Principles," and "Power Questions." He can be reached at http://andrewsobel.com.

## Jerold Panas

Jerry is Executive Partner of Jerold Panas, Linzy & Partners, one of the world's most highly regarded firms in the field of fundraising services and financial resource development. His firm has served over 3,000 client institutions since its founding in 1968. Jerry's clients include many of the foremost non-profit institutions in the world. They include every major university, museum, and health care center in the United States. Internationally, Jerry has advised organizations as diverse as the University of Oxford, The American Hospital of Paris, and Nuestros Pequeños Hermanos Mexico, the largest orphanage in the world.

Jerry is the author of 15 popular books, including the all-time bestsellers *Asking* and *Mega Gifts*. He is founder and chairman of the board of the Institute for Charitable Giving, one of the most significant providers of training in philanthropy.

Because of the prominence of the firm and the impact of Jerry's writing, few have had a greater influence in the history of the profession. He is a favorite speaker at conferences and workshops across the nation. He gives over 50 keynote speeches a year with a variety of titles, including "Shaking the Money Tree," "Be the Best You Can Be," "The Magic Partnership," "Listen!" and "I Hear a Gift, Aim High." He can be reached at http://jeroldpanas.com.